Taunton's

Taunton's

NEW Kitchen

IDEA BOOK

HEATHER J. PAPER

The Taunton Press

To Russ and DesiLu

The Taunton Press, Inc.
63 South Main Street, PO Box 5506
Newtown, CT 06470-5506
e-mail: tp@taunton.com

Editors: Peter Chapman, Christina Glennon
Copy editor: Candace B. Levy
Jacket/Cover design: Kimberly Adis
Interior design: Kimberly Adis
Layout: Sandra Mahlstedt
Illustrators: Christine Erikson p. 26; Joanne Kellar Bouknight pp. 61, 85, 89, 157
Cover photographers: Front cover: Mark Lohman (main image & bottom right), Randy O'Rourke (top right)
                    Back cover: Mark Lohman (all photos)

Fine Homebuilding® is a trademark of The Taunton Press, Inc., registered in the U.S. Patent and Trademark Office.

The following names/manufacturers appearing in *New Kitchen Idea Book* are trademarks: Barroca™, CaesarStone®, Energy Star®, Forest Stewardship Council®, National Kitchen & Bath Association℠, Realtor®

Library of Congress Cataloging-in-Publication Data

Names: Paper, Heather J., author.
Title: New kitchen idea book / Heather J. Paper.
Description: Newtown, CT : The Taunton Press, Inc., 2016.
Identifiers: LCCN 2016016791 | ISBN 9781631864063
Subjects: LCSH: Kitchens.
Classification: LCC NA8330 .P37 2016 | DDC 690/.44--dc23
LC record available at https://lccn.loc.gov/2016016791

Printed in the United States of America
10 9 8 7 6 5 4 3 2 1

acknowledgments

It's hard to know where to start thanking all of the people responsible for this book. My name may be on the cover but, if you'll pardon the pun, that's not the whole story.

My first shout-out must go to Peter Chapman, Executive Editor at The Taunton Press. I appreciate beyond words the confidence he showed in my tackling the vastly popular subject of kitchens. The opportunity to look at kitchens from every angle and to teach the reader important lessons resulted in my coming away with more knowledge myself.

My sincere thanks go, as well, to the rest of the Taunton team. I couldn't have asked for a better editor to work with than Christina Glennon, nor a more organized art director than Rosalind Loeb Wanke. My thanks go to Katy Binder, too, for keeping track of such a massive number of photographs. Every author should be so lucky as to work with such a cohesive team.

Those responsible for this book also include numerous others, including the professionals represented on these pages. They exemplify creativity beyond imagination. In my mind's eye I see an architect or kitchen designer sitting down with a homeowner, sketching an idea on nothing more than a paper napkin. A germ of an idea is soon detailed to the nth degree, and then translated into reality by builders, contractors, interior designers, and craftsmen. Thank you all for generously sharing your work with us.

A huge shout-out goes, too, to the photographers who provided top-notch images for this book. Thanks to Mark Lohman, Ryann Ford, Randy O'Rourke, and Undine Prohl for investing their time to locate extraordinary kitchens. But kudos go to others, as well; please reference the credits at the back of the book for the names of photographers—and design professionals—for individual images.

Finally, I want to thank my husband, Russ, whose love and support mean more than he will ever know. I may have studied my profession in the ranks of journalism school but his unwavering belief has made me the writer I am today.

contents

introduction

I CAN TELL YOU PRECISELY WHEN my love affair with the kitchen began. I was just tall enough to see over the counter, but it was enough to be able to watch my mother and grandmothers work their magic. Seeing them roll out biscuits or fry chicken was only the beginning of my admiration, though; the smells that wafted through the kitchen left me in pure awe.

Admittedly, I didn't give as much thought to the kitchen per se as I did to the mouth-watering food that came out of it. That was, until I had one of my own. My first kitchen, for instance, took efficiency to the nth degree. Tucked behind a folding door in my studio apartment, it featured Lilliputian-size appliances, and if I stretched my arms, I could touch the walls on both ends. Since then, I've been in search of *the* perfect kitchen—one that is comfortable to work in, has up-to-the-minute appliances, and is inviting to friends

and family. Admittedly, I'm still in search of that dream kitchen, and if you picked up this book, chances are you are, too.

There's no denying that designing your dream kitchen can be overwhelming, even if you have a good idea of your preferences. That's why, on these pages, we'll take you through the process step by step. Whether you're self-assured or a bit unsettled when it comes to kitchen design, this book is certain to take you to the next level. It's filled with information and inspiration, providing guidance for everything from smart floor plans to cabinetry, countertops, and appliances. Some ideas presented within these pages may have never occurred to you while others might solidify those of your own. But that's all a part of the process. There is no one right solution; rooms are constantly evolving, as tastes and family dynamics change.

Before planning your new kitchen, though, it's important to take a step back, to take a good look at your present-day space. What do you love about it? What do you not? The process can be as simple as making a list of pros and cons, with those items or aspects that you love under pros and those that you don't under cons. If your list of pros is on the short side, it may be an indication that a total renovation is in order. If, on the other hand, your list of pros is long, perhaps all you need are a few tweaks here and there.

As you shop for the new elements of your dream kitchen, be sure to consider all of the alternatives. Long gone are the days when in-store purchases were your only option. Shopping online puts a plethora of choices at your fingertips—all in the comfort of your own home. Check out showrooms for discounted floor models as well as seasonal sales. (To find the best deals on appliances, for instance,

shop in January, September, or October, when manufacturers are rolling out new models.)

Finally, while making each decision along the way, be sure to balance beauty with function. Even the most efficient, hard-working kitchen won't be inviting to work in if it lacks your personal sense of style.

layout and style

● ● ●

THE KITCHEN IS A MAGNET IN ANY HOME. IT DRAWS THE FAMILY together for daily meals, and whether you're entertaining large groups or small, guests always seem to end up in the kitchen. It's where you can sit down to catch up on bills and where kids can hang out to do homework. Because it works hard in so many ways, the kitchen takes plenty of planning, and thanks to the requisite sinks, cabinets, and appliances, it commands more money per square foot than any other room in the house.

Given the amount of time spent in the kitchen, comfort and style should be high priorities. What look makes you feel most at home? Don't get swept up in the latest fads, unless they're a good fit for your personal needs. A "hot" color, for instance, may appeal to you now, but you may grow tired of it in a year or two. On the other hand, the current trend toward energy efficiency is one that will make you—and your budget—happy forever.

If there's one thing more important than how a kitchen looks, though, it's how the room works. Does it need to accommodate one cook or two? Would an extra-tall island better suit your height? Start designing your space by using a work triangle that connects—with imaginary lines—the sink, range, and refrigerator, keeping the distance from one to the next no more than 9 ft. Then tweak the plan to make the kitchen work best for you. The result will be an efficient layout with well-placed appliances and equipment that will ease your daily routine, saving countless steps along the way.

In this handsome kitchen, a commercial-quality black range is surrounded by dark, distressed cabinetry topped with luxe white Carrara marble. The island, meanwhile, is the perfect counterpoint of lighter wood with a darker counter.

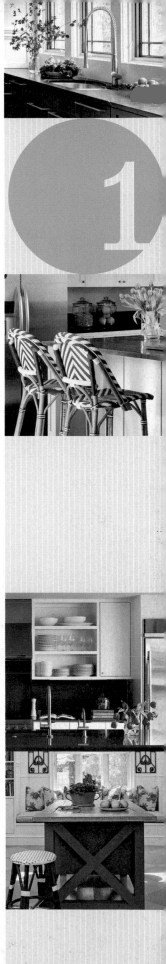

what's your style?

●●● PERHAPS YOU HAVE A CLEAR VISION OF your ideal kitchen. A traditionalist might opt for dark walnut cabinetry and striking granite countertops. A modernist, on the other hand, might prefer white laminate cabinets teamed with hard-as-rock maple counters. If you're undecided about your personal style, try this simple exercise: Thumb through this book and magazines, looking for rooms that you find appealing; there are sure to be some common aspects that will give you a sense of where to start. Look for qualities that identify a particular style, such as the warmth and simplicity of a country-style kitchen or the sophistication that contemporary kitchens can convey. Don't be surprised if you find that you like a variety of styles; an eclectic approach can be one of the best ways to put your personal stamp on a room.

FACING PAGE Light finishes throughout this transitional kitchen—from the limestone floor to the beamed ceiling—not only keep the space open and airy but also allow the focus to stay squarely on the stunning ocean view just beyond.

RIGHT Everything about this kitchen characterizes it as traditional, from the cabinetry to the pendant fixtures to the pair of barstools. The seafoam green scheme, though, gives it a fresh twist, making it all the more inviting.

ABOVE Country can take many forms, including a cottage-style kitchen like this. The all-white area feels clean and crisp, while pale blue touches—in the dishes, pendant fixtures, and nearby easy chair—keep things on the soft side.

ABOVE This kitchen has a contemporary attitude, starting with its black frame-and-panel cabinetry. That stance goes a step further on the room's outer wall, where open shelving is used in lieu of conventional cabinets, creating a greater sense of space in the process.

more about...
INSPIRATION POINTS

more often than not, you'll find one "must-have" element for your kitchen. Perhaps it's a stunning slab of stone or exquisite cabinetry. So let that element be the style springboard for the rest of the room. Choose colors that complement your particular item or materials that offer an eye-catching contrast. For example, that slab of stone—transformed into countertops—will stand out beautifully against a more subdued backsplash. As for cabinets, they can be prime purveyors of a kitchen's style; you'll find designs that run the gamut from time-honored traditional to the utmost in contemporary. Once you've made your selection, let the cabinets' character guide the rest of your kitchen decisions. Don't think, however, that your motivation needs to come from a major element; even the smallest of details—such as knobs and pulls—can inspire that first design decision.

As a rule, wood cabinetry conjures up thoughts of traditional style, but this kitchen proves that the material is equally at home in contemporary spaces. White subway tile and Carrara marble surfaces provide a stunning contrast, allowing the wood's rich grain to take center stage.

ABOVE At first glance, stream-lined cabinetry seems to signal this kitchen as contemporary. A closer look, though, reveals its transitional persona. Rattan chairs at the breakfast area have a traditional history, as do the glass-fronted cabinets flanking the cooktop.

RIGHT Everything about this kitchen identifies it as traditional, from the frame-and-panel cabinets to the subway-tiled backsplash. Subtle variations of neutral hues throughout the room, however, give it a sophisticated, up-to-date style.

•tips on trends

Trends are exciting. Who doesn't want the latest thing? But they make sense in your kitchen only if they fit your personal style—or if you're comfortable with the fact that trends can quickly come and go. Cabinet trends change more slowly than others, in part because cabinets are such big-ticket items. According to the National Kitchen & Bath Association℠ (NKBA), perennially popular cherry cabinets are starting to see competition from clean-lined contemporary styles. In terms of color, white is the most common color scheme, followed by gray. And color-blocked kitchens—two distinct hues in the same space—are growing in popularity. Finally, while country style isn't as prevalent as it once was, mixing rustic and contemporary elements is a fresh take on the theme.

Trends are not solely about fashion, either. Today's function-based fads include specialty appliances like steam ovens and wine refrigerators, flat-screen TVs and docking stations, and even multiples of the same appliance—from ovens and cooktops to refrigerators. One of the most important kitchen trends, though, is to consider the needs of *all* users and, yes, that includes pets.

ABOVE RIGHT Mixing rustic and contemporary elements is one of today's hottest trends as is color blocking, using two distinct hues in a room. This kitchen covers both with one fell swoop with its blue contemporary cabinetry and reclaimed wood accents.

RIGHT Contemporary kitchens continue to gain in popularity, exemplified by the straightforward styling of this room. White lacquer cabinetry sets the modern mood; the rest of the room is decked out in equally uncomplicated maple, the pale wood adding a touch of warmth.

TOP Doubling up on appliances makes sense in a two-cook kitchen, and this one takes the concept one step further. A sink—with plenty of prep space—on each side of the island ensures both cooks can work unencumbered.

BOTTOM There's no hard-and-fast rule that every-thing has to match in a kitchen. In fact, contrasting colors are on the rise. This kitchen highlights that trend beautifully, teaming dark base cabinets with the cream-colored wall cabinets and island.

more about...
RESALE VALUE

he average kitchen sees some kind of makeover every 15 years, more extensive remodels tend to happen during a strong economy and lighter redos when money is tight. When planning any kind of kitchen renovation, homeowners—especially those planning to move in the next few years—often consider what kind of kitchen will sell, specifically when it comes to kitchen trends that are hot on the market. While an investment of any kind might give you a decent return, keep this in mind: National trends aren't as important as what sells in *your* neighborhood, so consult a local Realtor® to find out what's selling in your area. But remember that this will be your kitchen, no matter how long or short a time, so be sure it's one that you will enjoy.

style directions

●●● PERSONAL STYLE IS MORE IMPORTANT than you might think; surrounding yourself with familiar and favorite things not only gives you something pleasant to look at but is also uplifting. A traditionalist, for instance, may prefer time-honored frame-and-panel cabinetry, perhaps topped with transom glass. Country style, meanwhile, is traditional in its own right but definitely more relaxed and laid-back. Modern/contemporary kitchens are typically identified by their streamlined flat-panel cabinetry and sleek backsplashes. And transitional or eclectic kitchens are best suited for those who want a mix of styles. Transitional kitchens subtly blend a variety of styles while eclectic kitchens are deliberate mashups.

According to the NKBA, transitional/eclectic and contemporary kitchens are currently in vogue. Their rise in popularity can be credited in part to the fact that homeowners are no longer afraid to mix and match, creating a look that's truly their own. Meanwhile, the draw of contemporary kitchens is their soothing, streamlined look. That's not to say that traditional style doesn't still have its fair share of devotees or country style, either, for that matter. It all comes down to what speaks to you, what you'll be comfortable with on a day-to-day basis.

This traditional kitchen may not have an overabundance of square footage, but some smart design decisions make it live larger than its dimensions. An all-white scheme opens up the space as do untreated windows that seemingly extend the kitchen to the outdoors.

RIGHT Traditional elements are the order of the day in this kitchen, with the range of rustic to refined keeping things interesting. Handsome frame-and-panel cabinetry sets the tone, and the casual barstools and rough-hewn beams provide variety.

more about...
COST CONSIDERATIONS

*i*f you were to look, side-by-side, at a clean-lined contemporary kitchen and a traditional version with intricate carvings and moldings, the natural conclusion would be that the contemporary one would be cheaper, right? After all, there's less going on. On the contrary, those crisp edges and perfectly flush surfaces in the contemporary kitchen take time and precision to achieve. In most cases, trimming a joint requires more material but is less labor-intensive than finishing the joint itself. That said, cabinetry and trim are available in a wide variety of profiles and materials, so it's a sure bet you can get the look you like within the constraints of your budget.

ABOVE Stainless-steel cabinetry gives this kitchen a contemporary, industrial-chic appearance, but the traditional marble backsplash and island countertop reel it right back into the transitional category.

LEFT Base cabinets are painted gray in this transitional kitchen, keeping them firmly grounded. Meanwhile, everything above counter level is white, making the room seem taller and making the ceiling all but disappear into thin air.

BELOW Rich cherry cabinetry, crown moldings, and granite countertops place this kitchen definitively in the traditional style. A few contemporary elements, however—including pendant lights over the island and a stainless-steel backsplash behind the range—result in an overall transitional feeling.

quick fixes...
FOR STYLE

ⓘ f budget constraints don't allow for a major kitchen redo, think small. Even minor changes can make a major difference.

- New hardware can freshen cabinets, as can repainting doors, drawer faces, and cabinet interiors.

- Fresh paint, one of the most inexpensive options you'll find, can do wonders on walls and trim.

- Up the style ante by tiling over a drywall backsplash; just be sure there's enough depth for the extra thickness.

- Replace a flush-mounted light fixture over an island with a chandelier for an added touch of glamour. Use one large fixture, or two or three in a row.

LEFT Contemporary style is often thought of as hard edged, but the wood cabinetry in this kitchen conveys an element of warmth. Because using it exclusively throughout the room could have been too much of a good thing, a Carrara marble island and hood provide a welcome contrast.

•traditional

Traditional kitchens come in many incarnations but they all have one thing in common: They are based on architectural details of bygone eras, for the most part before the mid-20th century. Generally, traditional kitchens will have more ornate moldings than their modern counterparts while cabinetry will feature frame-and-panel doors. Specific styles call for specific details too, such as inset quartersawn oak doors on Craftsman-style cabinets. But don't assume that all traditional kitchens are basic brown; more and more homeowners are mixing cabinet colors. Cream-colored perimeter cabinets might be teamed with a dark espresso island. Or a kitchen with dark-stained cabinetry might feature accents of deep blue. No matter how you mix things up, the result will be a fresh take on tradition.

ABOVE The boundaries between traditional and country style can sometimes become blurred, especially when there are elements of each. While gingham patterns and pewter accessories speak of country in this room, it's the raised-panel cabinetry, intricate trimwork, and even the Windsor chairs that identify it as traditional.

LEFT A close look at this traditional kitchen reveals how cabinetry defines specific work zones. Cream-colored cabinets surround the sink and the dishwasher around the corner to the right. Meanwhile, the range is flanked by darker drawers, and the color is picked up in the island.

ABOVE This kitchen pares traditional style down to its purest form; elements were chosen for their clean lines, giving each equal importance. There's just enough color and pattern in the predominantly white kitchen, as well, to keep things visually interesting.

LEFT White is still the most common color scheme for kitchens, and this traditional example keeps it simple. Minimal touches of pattern and color can be found in the mullioned upper cabinets and the blue seat cushions on the schoolhouse-style barstools.

•country

Country-style kitchens have a casual look, one that's instantly warm and welcoming. Their interpretations can be wide-ranging, but all country kitchens harken back to an earlier era in some way. French Country, English country, and Tuscan style were inspired by rural life in their respective geographic areas. And American country has various translations of its own, typically characterized by muted colors and worn finishes—from distressed cabinetry to slate or butcher-block countertops. Incorporate a farmhouse sink or a brick backsplash to capture the country spirit in your kitchen. Or use white finishes and feminine details to create a cottage style. Whatever direction you take your country style, it's sure to be inviting.

ABOVE Wormwood cabinetry gives this kitchen a country bent, albeit a sophisticated one. The soft taupe color of the storage units blends in beautifully with the rest of the room's neutral hues. Plus their casual styling is the perfect partner for the concrete sink.

BELOW This kitchen typifies country in every way, from the wide-plank wood floors to the cabinetry, with wood knobs and legs that make it look like furniture. The rustic beams define the soaring vaulted ceiling.

This cottage-style kitchen gets its cheery attitude from a coral-colored island, a pale-blue range, a yellow-upholstered window seat, and a blue-and-green-checked floor to underscore it all. Meanwhile, white walls and cabinets keeps the bright colors from becoming overwhelming.

•contemporary

The terms *contemporary* and *modern* are often used interchangeably, but—in fact—they are two distinctly different styles. Modern style refers to a look rooted in the early to middle 20th century, while contemporary is a much broader term. It calls to mind sleek detailing, smooth surfaces, recessed lighting, and full flush doors in frameless cabinets, typically with simple drawers and doors. Gleaming materials—such as stainless steel, glass tile, and composites—may be the finishes of choice in a contemporary kitchen, carried out in monochromatic colors. But traditional materials and finishes can take on a contemporary point of view if designed with clean, linear details. In fact, it's not the material so much as the detailing that gives a kitchen a contemporary feel.

ABOVE The repetition of rectangular forms gives this kitchen a soothing sense of rhythm—first the cooktop surface, then the sink and, finally, the table and pair of benches. The minimal approach to all surfaces also speaks to contemporary styling.

ABOVE This small contemporary kitchen makes the most of every inch. Taking advantage of the wall between the kitchen and the adjacent living area, the owner installed an oven as well as storage above and below.

RIGHT Proving that fashion and function can go hand in hand, this island is all but a work of art; the ventilation system, for instance, has a sculptural feeling. Plus the island is practically self-contained, including everything but the refrigerator.

BELOW A variety of gleaming surfaces—including stainless steel and high-gloss lacquer— are perfectly suited for this contemporary kitchen. A convenient pantry is defined by its bright red surround; swinging doors make it easily accessible.

•transitional

Transitional style allows you to have it all; it's a marriage of traditional and contemporary designs that results in a clean, classic look. If this sounds like your preferred style, you no doubt respect the craftsmanship and fine detailing of traditional elements but are also inspired by the pared-down approach of contemporary. So what's the secret to combining old and new? It's all about finding common ground in your room's components, so the disparate styles complement—rather than compete—with one another. Some styles, too, are transitional by their very nature. Shaker, for instance, is a prime example; it's timeless with lines so clean they come off as contemporary.

RIGHT Frame-and-panel doors and drawers are some of the most popular for traditional kitchens. This room, though, gives tradition a twist with the addition of industrial-chic accents in the barstools and lighting.

LEFT Overlay doors and drawers with a rich wood grain set a traditional tone in this kitchen. But more contemporary elements—like the barstools and even the diagonal design of the backsplash—make it unequivocally transitional.

ABOVE Beadboard cabinets and knotty wood are two archetypes of traditional style. But when they're teamed with contemporary elements like the barstools here, the result is a comfortable middle ground between traditional and contemporary.

LEFT The wood cabinetry of this kitchen could have steered it in a traditional direction. But the addition of modern stainless pulls changed the course; the hardware—plus a pair of contemporary barstools—brings it back to transitional styling.

layout: the triangle still makes sense

●●● THE CLASSIC KITCHEN TRIANGLE HAS THE range, the sink, and the refrigerator at its points. Ideally, the legs of that imaginary triangle—the total distance between the three points—will add up to no more than 27 ft. overall; as few as 12 ft. is fine in a small kitchen. But don't worry if your work triangle measures a few extra inches or even a few feet. Think of those measurements as guidelines to make your kitchen its most efficient— and to save you steps in the long run. It's not only the range, sink, and refrigerator that are important, however; give careful thought to their adjacent workspaces too. You'll need a landing space near the fridge, both a landing space and prep area near the cooktop, and room for dirty pots and pans next to the sink.

This galley kitchen features the sink on one side and all other appliances on the other. The result is a compact work triangle, one that requires just two or three steps from one work zone to another.

FOR LAYOUT

Without undertaking a complete renovation, there are plenty of function upgrades that can improve your kitchen's layout.

- Add cabinet inserts, such as lazy Susans, tilt-out bins, and wire racks.

- Remove fixed shelves, replacing them with pull-out versions that make items more easily accessible.

- Stuck with a kitchen that has too little counterspace? Add a freestanding butcher block–topped island in the center of the room.

- Create a more spacious feeling by removing a kitchen's upper cabinets on one or all walls. Replace them with easy-to-access open shelves or with nothing at all.

- Change out appliances without changing their location. You'll not only get a fresh new look but also more energy efficiency and all the latest bells and whistles, too.

ABOVE LEFT This U-shaped kitchen features a work triangle at its best; the double sink on one wall is centered between the range and refrigerator on the opposite. Though the short-legged triangle requires few steps, there's still room for two cooks to work.

LEFT Work triangles make a kitchen its most efficient, but this one takes the concept one step further; it puts the sink, range, and refrigerator all on one wall. Only the dishwasher—to the right of the main wash-up sink—is on another wall.

more about...
THE WORK TRIANGLE

an efficient kitchen comes down to smart geometry; a work triangle is an important element of both design and functionality. According to the National Kitchen and Bath Association, drawing an imaginary straight line from the sink to the cooktop to the refrigerator and back to the sink again forms that triangle. The sum of the work triangle's three sides should not exceed 27 ft., with each leg measuring between 4 ft. and 9 ft. No major traffic patterns should cut through

it, either. And if a kitchen has just one sink, it should be placed between or across from the cooking surface, food-prep area, or refrigerator.

That said, the basic triangle assumes that a kitchen will only have three major workstations—in a galley, U-shaped, or L-shaped kitchen—and a single cook.

But maybe, instead of a single range, your kitchen features a separate cooktop and wall ovens. Or a primary sink is supplemented by a prep or bar sink.

Even a refrigerator might be split into a separate fridge and freezer or supplemented by increasingly popular refrigerator drawers. When separate or secondary appliances are put into play, you may find that you have two work triangles; even so, it's still important to keep workstations in each no more than 4 ft. to 9 ft. apart. And there's a real bonus in doubling up on appliances, especially in a two-cook kitchen: Multiple appliances make it much easier to stay out of one another's way.

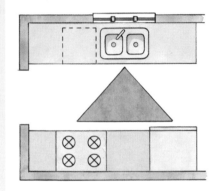

GALLEY KITCHEN

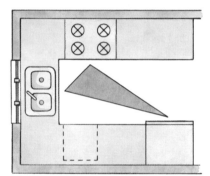

U-SHAPED KITCHEN

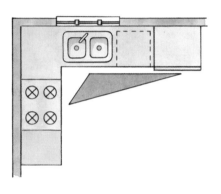

L-SHAPED KITCHEN

The beauty of this galley kitchen is that it's accessible from both ends. Still, it adheres to one hard-and-fast rule: There is no major traffic pattern that crosses its compact work triangle.

A bay window makes a U-shaped kitchen a natural. Here, the triangle from sink to range to refrigerator (opposite the island, not shown) has an added advantage: The island serves all three as a prep area and landing surface.

•sizing up your space

If you're a cook who has the kitchen all to yourself, you'll have plenty of room in a galley with a 38-in.-wide aisle. But if there's a second cook on a regular basis, you'll quickly grow tired of bumping into each other. If that's the case, make aisles 42 in. wide or, even better, 48 in. The extra width not only will permit passing room for both cooks but will also allow drawers, dishwasher, and refrigerator doors to be opened with ease. Plus you'll want to add even more space if one side of the aisle has bar seating. Family members and guests hanging out there, whether eating or just conversing with the cook, often want to get to the refrigerator or microwave. Your best bet is to place those appliances at the edge of the kitchen's heavy-duty workspace, instead of at the center.

ABOVE This city kitchen is the model of efficiency; it has a compact work triangle but still plenty of room for two cooks to work side by side. Not only does the eating bar let guests converse with the cooks but it also has a stunning view.

RIGHT When planning a kitchen, give plenty of thought to the width of the aisles. In a kitchen like this, for instance, allow space for someone to pass by while you're working at the sink or for another cook to open the oven door.

UNIVERSAL DESIGN

You've no doubt heard of universal design, also referred to as barrier-free design, aging-in-place design, or accessible design. What you may not be aware of, however, is that it has less to do with age, health, or ability and more to do with simple common sense. To incorporate the concept into your kitchen consider these tips:

- Aisles should be at least 42 in. wide—48 in. is even better—for a two-cook work area, providing a 5-ft.-dia. clear space somewhere to allow a wheelchair to turn around.
- Opt for a movable island instead of a fixed one or supplement a fixed island with a rolling cart. A movable island can be pushed aside in an instant to make room for a walker or wheelchair and can double as a buffet table too.
- Choose full-extension hardware for drawers and pull-out shelves to make storage more accessible.
- For drawers, select easy-to-grip pulls and knobs instead of streamlined pull cylinders and tabs. For doors, lever handles are easier to operate than knob handles.

- Provide countertops of different heights to make a variety of kitchen tasks easier. It is, for instance, more comfortable to knead and roll out dough on lower surfaces while some fine motor tasks—such as using small appliances—are easier on higher services.
- A shallow sink is easier to reach into than a deep one; likewise, a single-lever faucet is simpler to operate than a two-handle faucet.
- When it comes to appliances, configurations and elevations make a difference. A side-by-side refrigerator is easier to access than any other configuration except for refrigerator and freezer drawers, although drawers are more expensive per cubic foot. In terms of ovens, a wall oven is easier to operate than a range oven because it is elevated above the floor but a microwave oven is easier and safer to access when it is located lower.
- Keep flooring smooth—think hardwood or solid vinyl, for instance—and avoid using apt-to-slip throw rugs.
- Provide lighting for every work surface, not only to make the space brighter and more cheerful but to make it safer too.

Universal design is at every turn in this New England kitchen. There's plenty of space for a wheelchair to pass behind the Windsor-style barstools. Plus a hardwood floor allows easy accessibility to the dining area, where a conventional chair can be pulled away to make room for a wheelchair.

•seamless transitions

Thanks to elements that are just as fashionable as they are functional, the kitchen is no longer relegated to second-class rank; more often than not, it has the same high-style status as the rest of the house. As a result, it's easier than ever to create a cohesive relationship between it and the adjacent living spaces. Your strategy can be as simple as carving out a pass-through or widening a doorway or as complex as creating a giant great room that includes both living and dining spaces. Or reserve a corner for a handy home office. Whether the adjacent space you create is large or small, be sure the result is a seamless transition. Spaces do not have to match exactly but should blend with similar materials and/or colors. And what if you want to hide large appliances? Most can be concealed behind panels that match the cabinetry.

FACING PAGE TOP
When it's time to set the dining table in this great room, dinnerware—stored in the open shelves of the island— is conveniently close at hand. The beamed ceiling and French doors that the kitchen and dining area share get much of the credit for the unified feeling.

ABOVE A partial wall can create a separation of space and still allow visual continuity between kitchen and living areas. This half-wall is just big enough to serve as the perfect place for two diners, for kids to do homework, or for guests to chat up the cook.

RIGHT Creating a connection between the kitchen and living area can be as simple as a pass-through or as complex as melding them into a single space. The beauty of this great room is that the kitchen area gets the benefit of the living room's tall windows and the fireplace too.

•connecting with the outdoors

A great view is an asset to any kitchen. Not only does it add to the room's natural appeal but oversize windows and doors visually blur the boundaries between indoors and out, making your kitchen seem larger in the process. Over the sink, for instance, an uninterrupted window—with no mullions—will offer a clear view. And while a pair of French doors opening to the patio can be charming, three pairs triple the impact. The bonus of easy access to the outdoors is that it also makes entertaining easier. Guests can move effortlessly between indoors and out, which just might make the cook happier too: There will invariably be fewer people in the kitchen.

RIGHT Diners at the island in this kitchen get the full benefit of the view beyond, not only straight ahead to the backyard but—through the slanted glass at the top of the window—also to the treetops.

FACING PAGE TOP The view through a floor-to-ceiling window wall allows the homeowners to see for miles. The abundance of natural light is a bonus for anyone working in the kitchen.

FACING PAGE BOTTOM With its slanted ceiling, this kitchen—especially if given window treatments—could have easily seemed closed in. Instead, the white-painted cabinetry and ceiling fade into the backdrop, with dark ceiling beams directing the eye toward the stunning view beyond the windows.

kitchen islands

IF THE KITCHEN IS THE HEART OF ANY HOUSEHOLD, THE ISLAND TAKES it one step further; it's the core of the kitchen. Its function may be singlefold or multipurpose. Some owners might want a dedicated workspace while others may need a spot to accommodate food prep, cooking, eating, *and* entertaining.

Thus it's no surprise that there is no perfect island. It's up to you, your budget, and the available space to decide its size, contents, and materials. A simple kitchen table may be all you need—or have room for; you can sit down to work or stand up and it's the perfect height for kneading bread. More often than not, though, the kitchen island contains loads of storage, an appliance or two, and offers an eating bar as well.

While it's important that your island complement the rest of the kitchen, don't think that it has to match exactly. To make your island look distinct from the rest of the room's cabinetry, use a different wood or the same wood in a different color or finish. Another way to change things up is to use a different material entirely than the perimeter cabinets. Serious chefs might opt for stainless-steel countertops to allow for plenty of durable food-prep space. You might even use more than one countertop material, to create specialized work zones. Butcher block is a good choice for food prep, while marble is ideal for baking.

A freestanding coral island is the focal point of this cottage-style kitchen, but it's just as functional as it is fashionable. A butcher-block top provides a large food-prep surface while drawers and doors serve up plenty of storage.

No matter the size of your kitchen island—though it's best to have nothing smaller than a 3-ft. by 4-ft. working area— keep surrounding traffic patterns in mind. There should be at least 42 in. of space between the island and the outside edge of the cabinetry, 48 in. if there are typically multiple cooks.

built-in islands

● ● ● A BUILT-IN ISLAND CAN BE A SIMPLE assemblage of base cabinets with the countertop of your choice, but it can also be all but a self-contained kitchen—including a sink, cooktop and oven, and even warming and refrigerator drawers. These kinds of major appliances, of course, require plumbing, wiring, and possibly ductwork. Plus built-in islands require electrical outlets at code-required locations, which can make your island more efficient. Give some thought to which small appliances you'll use at the island and where, then store them conveniently close to those outlets.

By no means are all islands rectangular, nor are they all one-level, either. A two-level island countertop might incorporate a food-prep area and a stepped-up eating bar. And a three-level island isn't out of the ordinary, either, with specific zones for food prep and dining, as well as a lower surface for, say, kneading bread—making it an ergonomically good choice. But a one-level countertop, with no interrupting sink or appliance, isn't without its advantages too. It makes the perfect surface for holiday baking or for laying out a buffet.

While the perimeter cabinets are crafted of dark cabinetry and marble, the island complements them with its cream-colored paint and wood countertop. The polished wood surface conveys the look of fine dining, further enhanced by the upholstered chairs.

A tough-as-nails work surface makes this built-in island hardworking, but the butcher-block surfaces on both ends make it even more so. Doubling up on the cutting boards makes this the perfect two-cook kitchen.

more about...
SIZING UP ISLANDS

make no mistake: The size of a kitchen island requires some thought. The first consideration should be the amount of space between your island and the perimeter cabinets. A single-cook aisle can be 42 in. wide but if there are typically two cooks working at once, a 46-in. to 60-in. aisle will be easier for both to navigate. A wider space is important, too, when appliance doors open into the aisle. A 60-in. distance is also a good rule of thumb between an island and an adjacent dining table; dining chairs at the table and/or barstools at the island will need room to be pulled out. Although the standard countertop height is 36 in., your island can be as low or as high as you like. Give some thought to whether cooking, dining, or both is most important to you, keeping in mind that you can have it all with a two-level countertop. Or instead of one large island, perhaps two smaller ones make sense. Finally, in terms of placement, avoid interrupting two points of the kitchen triangle; you don't, for example, want to have to walk around your island to get from the sink to the refrigerator.

In this spacious kitchen, one long island would have meant many more steps for the cook to get from point A to point B. But dividing the island into two parts multiplies the efficiency. Plus—when extra seating is needed—there's still room to add a table for four at one end.

more about...
ISLAND LIGHTING

a balanced mix of lighting is essential in any room, and the kitchen is no exception. Combining ambient, task, and accent lighting—including recessed, ceiling-mount, undercounter, and even natural light—provides a comfortable feeling. When designing your island, think specifically about how it will be used. If dining will be its primary purpose, ambient light in the form of one beautiful fixture may be all diners need to see what they're eating. If, on the other hand, your island will be a workspace, safety is an essential part of the equation. Pendants are often used above islands because they provide concentrated task lighting on any work surface.

A pair of blue pendant lights is eye-catching in this kitchen, picking up the room's accent hue. More important, the fixtures provide sufficient light for the island below—a prep sink with workspaces on both sides of it.

Pendant lights are a popular option for islands, but be sure to keep proper proportion in mind. This long island calls for fixtures large enough to shed light on the entire work surface—especially because there's a cooktop in the mix.

ABOVE This island incorporates a convenient cooktop, surrounded by commercial-quality stainless steel. A stepped-up glass surface is the perfect height for an eating bar, keeping diners out of harm's way from the cooktop's splatters and steam.

LEFT There's no hard-and-fast rule that islands must be rectangular in shape. This one is rounded on one end, making it easier for diners to interact with one another.

•island storage

The kitchen island is capable of being the workhorse of a kitchen, especially when it comes to storage; it can practically double the space found in perimeter cabinets. It's the perfect place for all manner of open and closed storage, from cabinets and drawers to fixed and pull-out shelves. What's more, island storage is easy to reach. Depending on the size and style of your island, it may not be possible to include storage on all four sides. If that's the case, you can finish nonstorage sides with decorative panels that match or complement the rest of the cabinetry. To improve efficiency, keep cooking gear on the food-prep side and dinnerware on the living/ dining side, or at least on the ends. And when designing your island, keep in mind that—while a curved island can make for smoother traffic patterns—curved cabinetry is expensive. However, there's a simple solution: Place a curved counter on top of conventional cabinets.

It's not always possible to incorporate storage on the living/ dining side of an island. But this one carves out a sliver of space at each end; the open shelves are handy for cookbooks and treasured collectibles.

ABOVE LEFT The stainless-steel base of this island matches the rest of the room's cabinetry, and its marble top is perfectly suited for baking. Drawers tucked into the end of the island are a smart choice too; they can be accessed without getting in the way of the cook or the diners.

ABOVE Pull-out shelves beneath the cooktop in this island keep pots and pans conveniently close. And because they're not concealed behind cabinet doors, access is even easier.

LEFT Proof that an island need not match the perimeter cabinets, this reclaimed-wood model is an arresting contrast to the rest of the room's sleek white cabinetry. There is an element of continuity, though; both have the same sleek countertops.

•island sinks

A sink—be it the main wash-up sink or a smaller prep style—can turn an island into a handy food-prep area, especially if it's near the refrigerator and cooktop; the combination of elements can provide an efficient work triangle. Likewise, a sink located in an island can make clean up convenient. Give careful thought, though, as to the sink's location; you may want to shift it to one end or the other rather than centering it, which leaves two smaller workspaces instead of one large one. Consider too the type of sink you'll choose. A prep sink, by design, has a smaller profile, making it less visible. A large wash-up sink, on the other hand—especially one with an adjacent dishwasher— is apt to put dirty dishes in plain view. Consider a stepped-up countertop on the living/dining side, one that will hide any disorder while providing bar seating.

ABOVE A gleaming white farmhouse-style sink is centered on the lower level of this island. It's the primary wash-up sink but any dirty dishes that get stacked next to it are out of view from the adjacent living/dining area.

LEFT In a large kitchen, a sink in the island next to a work surface not only can be a convenience but can save precious steps along the way. This island eases cleanup, with a dishwasher to the right of the sink and paper towels on the left.

FACING PAGE This two-tier island features a sink on the lower level, creating a designated wash-up zone that also keeps splashes to a minimum for nearby diners.

•island appliances

A central island is perfectly appropriate for appliances, especially undercounter types such as microwaves, warming ovens, and refrigerators. But there are some guidelines to keep in mind. First, be aware that appliance doors will open into the aisle, so leave room to open them and still allow people to pass easily. If you opt for a cooktop, include a heatproof landing space—at least 15 in. on each side and a broader expanse on the back, or a raised countertop. A higher countertop offers not only protection from splatters and steam but also a place to plate a meal. For those cooktops, a pop-up exhaust system is one option, but a range hood is more efficient and provides the kind of task lighting that a cook requires. Whatever appliances you want to incorporate, though, make your choices early in the design process; those choices will affect every other decision.

ABOVE RIGHT The model of a productive work area, this blue-painted island incorporates an oven and microwave under the counter, delegating the only remaining sliver of space to drawer storage for utensils and other cooking essentials.

RIGHT Secondary sinks and appliances—like this prep sink and warming oven—are a good choice for an island, given their typically small size. Here, the warming oven opens to an extra-wide aisle, so people can pass easily, even when the door is open.

In a two-cook kitchen, it pays to double up on appliances—and sometimes islands too. This contemporary kitchen devotes one island to a cooktop and undercounter appliances and another to a workspace and eating bar.

freestanding islands

● ● ● A FREESTANDING ISLAND MAKES FOR A more flexible kitchen layout, a bonus if you like to move the workstation around from time to time or need to allow space for a wheelchair to pass. Freestanding islands may not be able to accommodate a sink or appliances, but the upside is that they're less costly. Still, they come with a variety of options. Many have wheels, like utility carts; just be sure, for safety's sake, they have locking features. A simple table can serve as an island too, and the bonus is that it provides a sit-down workspace. Even cabinetry to match the rest of your room can be topped with a counter and set on legs, much like a piece of furniture. One word of caution, however: Be sure any suspended light fixture over a freestanding piece is higher than your head for those times when you relocate the island.

The perfect height for a stand-up work surface, this island features a delicate turned-metal base that belies its hard-as-nails marble top. The see-through quality of the base makes it a good choice for close quarters, as it takes up little visual space.

This simple butcher-block island is positioned perfectly within this kitchen's work triangle, making it a touchstone among the refrigerator, range, and sink. The black-tipped legs are attention-getters, making it look more like a piece of furniture.

This butcher-block-topped table is the perfect fit for a cottage-style kitchen, providing not only a durable work surface but also drawer storage on each end. Plus it has the added bonus of being freestanding, giving it mobility within the room.

Butcher block is a natural choice for a country kitchen, but this workspace ups the ante with its multipurpose identity. Not only do casters make it moveable but it's also just the right height to enjoy a casual meal.

Don't let the understated styling of this island fool you; it's just as hardworking as the rest of the room. In addition to an expansive work surface, details such as storage drawers and a paper towel holder make all the difference.

SMALL SPACE SOLUTIONS

e ven if space is at a premium in your kitchen, you don't have to settle for less-than-sufficient workspace. A small drop-leaf table in the center of the room can increase your "counter space" at a moment's notice.

On a day-to-day basis, this rock-hard maple island serves as a handy workspace and cutting board. When needed, the drop leaf on one end can be extended to practically double the surface area. A stool or two can be pulled up for a casual meal or to simply chat with the cook.

dining and workspaces

• • •

DEDICATED SPACE FOR EATING IN OR NEAR THE KITCHEN SIMPLY makes sense. In-kitchen dining can be as casual as pulling a few stools up to a 36-in.-high island countertop, carving out space for a built-in nook, or simply making room for a freestanding table and chairs. If you opt for the latter and are wondering what table shape will best suit your room, look no further than the shape of the room itself. Rectangular and oval tables are best for long and narrow rooms, while round or square tables fit neatly into square-shaped spaces. All dining options have their advantages, but a freestanding table still offers the most flexibility. Wheelchairs and highchairs can be pulled up at a moment's notice, or—when needed—a freestanding table can be moved entirely out of the way.

In-room dining, however, shouldn't be your only consideration; think about how the space needs to work overall. Almost every family needs space to work at a computer or to pay household bills. And a place for kids to do supervised homework is a bonus. Ideally, these kinds of workspaces should be sheltered from high-intensity cooking, to keep projects safe from splashes and splatters, if nothing else. But quick

access is important, as well, just in case you're multitasking. Even a great view can present an opportunity; a bench beneath a window or a window seat in a bay might be just the place for meal planning, a quiet cup of coffee, or simply enjoying the scenery.

A diamond-patterned bench is tucked into one corner of this kitchen, its upholstered top concealing plenty of storage space. A pedestal table makes it easy for diners to get in and out, and armless chairs can add more seating as needed.

eat-in kitchens

● ● ● A FORMAL DINING ROOM IS PERFECT FOR dinner parties and holidays, but on an everyday basis, today's hectic schedules have made in-kitchen dining the norm. A simple table and chairs is still the go-to approach for many, their flexibility being the main draw. Chairs can be pulled away to create a buffet space or more can be added to accommodate a crowd. The popularity of built-in dining is on the rise; a cozy breakfast nook is often a favorite place to eat. As for bar seating, it's easily accessible, and barstools can be tucked away—or removed entirely—when the countertop is needed for food-prep or serving. If your kitchen has enough square footage, the best solution may be a combination of built-in and movable pieces that can adapt to your needs as they change daily.

No matter what eat-in dining option you choose, think beyond the table and its placement. How close do you want it to food prep? If it's too close, diners may have a tendency to get in the way. Think of your kitchen like any other prime real estate: It's all about location. Place an undercabinet refrigerator and/or microwave at the kitchen's perimeter where guests can grab cold drinks or warm up their coffee. They'll stay out of your cooking space, and you won't have to stop what you're doing to help them either.

FACING PAGE In this kitchen, dining can be as informal as pulling up a chair at the bar or as formal as sitting down for a full meal. The beauty of the bar seating is not only in the chairs' blue-and-white pattern but that the rattan pieces are lightweight, making them easy to move.

m ore than ever, pets are part of the family. So it makes sense that one of today's trends is to incorporate spaces throughout the house specifically for them. Four-legged members of the family often have in-kitchen eating areas, for instance. All that's needed is an out-of-the-way corner, where there's no danger of tripping over food and water bowls.

Kitchen floors are, out of necessity, easy to clean. It makes sense to locate your pet's feeding area there. This one makes the space extra special with a chalkboard that could be used for notes for the pet sitter.

ABOVE LEFT A round table is best for easy conversation; all of the diners can see one another. But the round shape of this space—and its tall glass doors and windows—has another advantage; it gives everyone a great view too.

LEFT On its own, the window seat in this kitchen would have been a comfortable place to take in the view. But a glass-top table and three rattan chairs turn it into a cozy eating area for four.

ABOVE A built-in table at the end of this kitchen island is teamed with four rattan chairs on a daily basis. When more seating is needed, a bench pulls up from a few feet away to accommodate two more.

RIGHT This painted table and chairs have cottage-style charm, blending well with the pale blues and greens of the walls and ceiling. The table is a hard worker too; the top can be expanded while a small drawer can hold napkins or other dining essentials.

it the perfect place for guests to enjoy hors d'oeuvres before dinner or to linger with coffee long after dessert is done. The combination of L-shaped built-in seating and conventional chairs adds to its flexibility.

more about...
THE IMPORTANCE OF ELBOW ROOM

to allow ample space for seated diners, the National Kitchen & Bath Association recommends 32 in. between the table or countertop edge and the nearest vertical wall or obstruction—if no through traffic passes behind them. If, however, traffic does pass behind seated diners, that dimension should be increased to 44 in.; 36 in. will work if you don't mind squeezing. For countertop height, depth, and width, see the chart below.

	COUNTER HEIGHT	KNEE-SPACE DEPTH	WIDTH PER SEAT	SEAT HEIGHT
Table dining	28 in. to 30 in.	18 in.	24 in.	18 in. to 19 in.
Standard countertop height	36 in.	15 in.	24 in.	24 in. to 26 in.
Bar height	42 in.	12 in.	24 in.	30 in.
Universal design access for wheelchair	27 in. to 34 in.	17 in. at feet 11 in. at knees	36 in.	N/A

•built-in dining

Built-in dining has an inherent cozy feeling, no matter what the configuration. It can be designed like a booth with two benches facing each other or with benches in an L- or U-shape. For booth and U-shaped seating, it's important to choose a pedestal table that won't interfere with diners getting in and out, while a four-legged table can be used with L-shaped seating. In either case, be sure that the table you choose is lightweight, so it can be moved easily for cleaning. There's something to be said as well for using a combination of built-in and chair seating around a freestanding table. Consider one with leaves that can be extended—and additional chairs pulled up—to serve more guests or to allow a wheelchair to be tucked in at the end. Finally, keep in mind that a built-in dining area will most likely be used for more than eating. If, for instance, the kids are apt to do homework there, be sure to provide electrical outlets.

ABOVE An L-shaped bench at the far end of this kitchen keeps a low profile; its back is no higher than the accompanying table. The result is a streamlined look in keeping with the kitchen itself.

LEFT Taking advantage of every inch, this built-in bench runs from the end of a cabinet bank all the way to the opposite wall. It tucks neatly beneath triple windows, teaming up with a glass-top table that takes up little visual space in close quarters.

The bay window in this kitchen is a natural spot for a U-shaped bench and accompanying table. The inside corners of the table are angled to match the shape of the upholstered seat, making it easier for diners to get in and out.

Chocolate-brown banquette seating and a dark wood table create a strong focal point in this contemporary kitchen. The bench's upholstered back adds extra comfort too, making it a favorite place well beyond mealtime.

A pedestal table makes this U-shaped dining area much easier to access. For built-in benches like this, a slight angular pitch on the back can up the comfort level, as can cushy throw pillows.

ABOVE AND RIGHT In a kitchen with precious little floor space, finding room for an eating area can be a challenge. The cabinet below this microwave, though, opens to reveal a drop-leg table just big enough for one or two. When mealtime is over, the lightweight chairs simply move back to the nearby dining room.

ABOVE Soaring walls in this niche are painted a bright orange, with a simple but striking wood bench at the base of each. The real attention-getter, however, is the table, artfully crafted from a single piece of wood.

RIGHT The L-shape of this built-in bench is softly rounded; the table picks up on the cue with its similar round shape. The beauty of this eating area is its location; cabinets full of dinnerware are within easy reach.

BUILDING IN COMFORT

A breakfast nook with benches requires a pedestal or trestle table, or—in a two-sided booth like this—the wall on one end and a central leg near the other can support the table.

THE TRADITIONAL BREAKFAST BOOTH

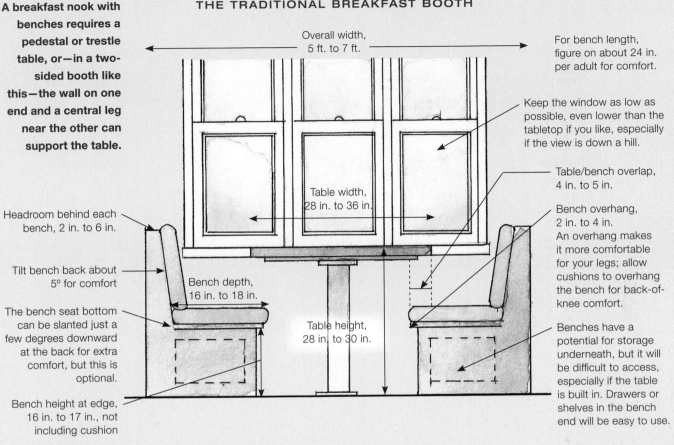

Overall width, 5 ft. to 7 ft.

For bench length, figure on about 24 in. per adult for comfort.

Keep the window as low as possible, even lower than the tabletop if you like, especially if the view is down a hill.

Table width, 28 in. to 36 in.

Table/bench overlap, 4 in. to 5 in.

Headroom behind each bench, 2 in. to 6 in.

Bench overhang, 2 in. to 4 in. An overhang makes it more comfortable for your legs; allow cushions to overhang the bench for back-of-knee comfort.

Tilt bench back about 5° for comfort

Bench depth, 16 in. to 18 in.

The bench seat bottom can be slanted just a few degrees downward at the back for extra comfort, but this is optional.

Table height, 28 in. to 30 in.

Benches have a potential for storage underneath, but it will be difficult to access, especially if the table is built in. Drawers or shelves in the bench end will be easy to use.

Bench height at edge, 16 in. to 17 in., not including cushion

OTHER WAYS TO CONFIGURE BUILT-IN DINING

Allow at least 32 in. to 36 in. between any wall cabinet and the end of the bench/edge of table.

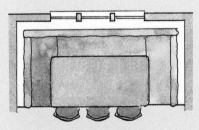

36-in. by 72-in. table with a bench on three sides

More bench seating allows for more sitters, especially if they are kid size.

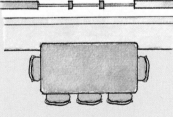

36-in. by 72-in. table with a single straight bench

This configuration is more flexible but may not fit quite as many people as the three-sided bench.

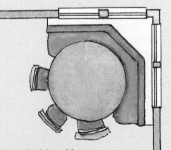

Round table with a corner bench

This configuration is both cozy and flexible. Note the angled corner; a square corner requires a square table.

The conventional approach might be to place a table parallel to a built-in, but this spot takes a different tack. A table placed at a right angle to the soft green bench gives head-of-the-table honors to one, or allows two to squeeze in side by side.

more about...
BUILT-IN STORAGE SPACE

built-in seating offers an opportunity for extra storage, but it's important to be practical about how it's used. A bin with a hinged top is a great place for items that are big or seasonal, such as picnic baskets or extra throws and pillows. Be sure, however, that it's easy to open the lid and to remove the items within. Plus if there are small children in the house, hinged-top bins should have safety catches or even be lockable, so little ones don't slam their fingers or aren't tempted to hide inside. Another option is to fit built-in seating with storage drawers. Those that open from the ends are most easily accessible but the drawers can face the accompanying table if it's lightweight and easy to move.

An L-shaped bench does double-duty in the corner of this kitchen, providing not only seating at the breakfast table but also storage in the pull-out bins below. The easy-to-move table and chairs make any one of the bins quickly accessible.

ABOVE Tucked just beneath a bank of tall windows, an L-shaped built-in bench proved to be the starting point for this inviting dining area. It can seat eight easily, thanks to the addition of three armless chairs and their slipcovered counterpart at one end.

LEFT This simple bench, in an L-shape, is painted white to blend with the rest of the room's trimwork. It's the perfect candidate for storage too; little-used or out-of-season items tuck neatly under the lids of the bench.

•bar seating

The breakfast bar is actually a misnomer; it's a great place to dine—or just hang out—any time of day. Side-by-side seating is ideal for diners who want to see what's cooking and to chat with the cook. It's a great place too for after-school snacks, where the kids can tell Mom or Dad all about their day. Meanwhile, L-shaped countertops make for more camaraderie; diners can converse with ease, and still watch what's going on in the kitchen. Whatever configuration you choose, it should be at least 18 in. deep. As for height, it should be somewhere between 36 in. and 48 in. (see p. 55 for specifics). And don't just buy barstools on the basis of looks; it's critical to match the bar height to the height of your stools and vice versa. Keep in mind too that stools are great for sliding under the countertop when not in use but chairs will give you more back support.

Acrylic barstools in this kitchen add a contemporary touch to an otherwise traditional surround. When not in use, they tuck neatly under the island—out of the way and all but out of view.

ABOVE Lemon-yellow bar seating adds a cheery touch to this kitchen. The stools' backs are just high enough to provide support but low enough to not interrupt the view to the kitchen.

RIGHT It's important that barstools be the right height for the eating bar—and vice versa. These industrial-chic versions solve the potential challenge beautifully; the wooden seats spin up or down according to the diner's height.

ABOVE A pass-through creates a connection between the kitchen and living room in this home. By extending the countertop on the living room side, an eating bar is created— complete with cream-colored stools that blend quietly with the wall color.

ABOVE These blue-and-white rattan barstools are eye-catching in an otherwise neutral kitchen. In addition to comfort, they possess another important quality; they're lightweight and easy to move around.

ABOVE The seats of these upholstered barstools have a slight dip, making them more comfy for diners. Because they have no backs, they tuck out of the way—under the island's overhang—when not needed.

LEFT The high backs of these barstools give them an extra element of support, as do the arms, for that matter. But the comfort doesn't stop there; strategically placed chrome rings provide foot rests.

These sculptural barstools are striking against the white-painted island. But their beauty is more than skin deep; the seats and backs are molded for the ultimate in comfort.

workspaces

●●● LONG GONE ARE THE DAYS WHEN THE kitchen served only as a place to cook meals and clean up after them. Today, it's the undisputed command post, where everything from homework to paying bills happens. Locating a workspace just outside the bounds of the kitchen proper is ideal; it allows multitasking while dinner is cooking. And all you really need is an out-of-the-way corner. Think first, though, about what tasks your workspace needs to handle. Does your family come and go at such a fast pace that you need a message board to keep track of it all? Consider a chalkboard, pin board, or magnet surface that needs no more than a sliver of space; you can even put one inside a tall cabinet door. A small desk too—even one just big enough for a laptop—is ideal for homework as well as menu planning. If you prefer to cook from recipe apps, keep a countertop stand handy for your digital tablet. Provide dedicated drawer space for charging cell phones, tablets, and laptops and, if possible, a base cabinet for an all-in-one printer. Having the basics close at hand, as well as an Internet connection, will make it easy for everyone in the family to work on their particular projects.

FACING PAGE Think about how your workspace will best suit you, then adjust accordingly. For this family, a desktop for one simply wasn't enough, so they tripled the space—and multiplied its efficiency too.

LEFT AND ABOVE Tucked out of the way at one end of the kitchen, this workspace has all the essentials, including a computer and shelves for cookbooks. Just around the corner is a full-length magnet board, to keep track of family goings-on and to display kids' art.

RIGHT Located at the end of a bank of cabinetry, this workspace is distinguished by its color. Although the cabinets in the corner office are the same style as those in the kitchen proper, here they're decked out in sage green.

BELOW All it took was a sliver of space in this pass-through to create a handy home office. In addition to the requisite computer, this work area features open shelves for oft-used items and closed cabinetry above for more storage.

ABOVE When a workspace is in or near a kitchen, don't hesitate to use the same cabinetry in both places. Here, the same white cabinets used in the kitchen around the corner provide storage space for home office essentials as well as serving pieces for the nearby dining area.

LEFT Although this workspace is just steps from the kitchen, its design makes it feel like a room unto itself. Simple in style, it has everything needed—from a laptop and comfortable chair to storage and adequate lighting.

cabinets

• • •

CABINETRY GETS TOP BILLING IN A KITCHEN, NOT ONLY BECAUSE
it sets the style and shapes your space but also because it demands a fair share
of your budget. So it's important to carefully consider all of your options, right
down to the last knob or pull. Because cabinets affect almost every other kitchen
component—from flooring to lighting—it's best to make cabinet decisions as early
as possible. Custom or semicustom cabinets can take time to construct, and even
stock cabinets may not be immediately available right off the shelf. As a rule, cabinets
are installed before almost everything else—appliances and countertops, even
backsplashes and sinks.

To make the entire process easier, get comfortable with cabinet terminology,
starting with cabinet case construction; do you prefer a face-frame or a frameless
case? Educate yourself on door and drawer types too, as well as hardware and
cabinet accessories. And get creative with configuration. Not all base and wall
cabinets have to match, and you may not want to fill an outside wall with cabinets if
they will block a great view. Once you've thought through every last decision, you're
ready to shop. You'll find a vast assortment of stock and semicustom cabinets or you
might opt to specify your own custom cabinetry. If you're a
do-it-yourselfer, and trying to keep costs down, don't forget
about knockdown (KD) and ready-to-assemble (RTA) options.

**Zebrawood is right
at home in this
contemporary kitchen.
Overlay doors and
drawers like these, with
a vertical grain, require
precise craftsmanship
and careful veneer
matching.**

configuring cabinetry

● ● ● WHEN CONFIGURING CABINETRY, IT'S only natural to visualize cabinets side by side, but also remember to look up. Consider how your cabinets will look from floor to ceiling too. Study elevations provided by your cabinetmaker to get a clear idea of the overall look or draw your own, for that matter. Give some thought as to how you want your kitchen to work, and then review the layout to be sure everything's covered. Standard base and wall cabinets may completely meet your needs, but there are other options; a tall china cabinet—perfect for serving pieces—might be located near the kitchen workspace yet be out of the way of the cook. Don't be concerned about perfectly lining up wall and base cabinets, either. Appliances and windows will invariably throw off the alignment. The good news is that a kitchen's backsplash, which provides a visual break, will make any less-than-perfect alignment inconspicuous.

ABOVE Flip-up frosted-glass doors on these wall cabinets offer a subtle view of their contents. Frameless base cabinets, flat-slab doors and drawers, and simple thumb pulls complete the contemporary look.

RIGHT The absence of wall cabinets makes this country-style kitchen seem even larger than its actual dimensions. The flat-slab drawers and frame-and panel doors are all punctuated by the same simple wood-knob hardware.

Face-frame cabinetry with frame-and-panel doors establish a conventional feeling in this kitchen. But the color scheme offers a fresh twist on tradition in the form of dramatic greens and blacks, inspired by the backsplash.

ABOVE This traditional kitchen features a mix of beaded-edge drawers and beaded-panel doors. While most of the cabinets are sage green, the one next to the window is glass fronted and painted white, so as not to overwhelm the window.

RIGHT The same cabinetry used in the nearby kitchen work zone was used for an out-of-the-way bar on this wall. Beaded frame-and-raised-panel doors and drawers in the base cabinets firmly ground their glass-fronted wall-hung counterparts.

Providing more storage space than a straight run would have, the base cabinets in this mid-century modern kitchen take an angular approach. Frameless wall cabinets and face-frame base cabinets all have the same easy-to-grab pulls.

more about...
BASE CABINETS

the standard base cabinet is just shy of 2 ft. deep and typically 34½ in. tall, allowing for a 1½-in. countertop and an overall height of 36 in. If you would like to vary either the depth or the height of the countertop, it is possible to specify taller or deeper cabinets. But there are other options. For extra height, you might set a standard case on a taller base. For more countertop depth, install standard cabinets a few inches away from the wall; in addition to extending the countertop all the way to the wall, be sure that any end gap is concealed with a panel that matches your cabinetry.

A mix of flat-slab and frame-and-panel drawers keep things interesting in this kitchen, though they all have the same black knobs in common. A matching cabinetry panel hides the dishwasher to the left; it's given a long pull to handle the weight.

In an otherwise white contemporary kitchen, this wall of wood cabinetry is an impressive focal point. The hardware on the frameless cabinetry is intentionally subtle, allowing the beauty of the wood to shine.

WALL CABINETS

Wall cabinets aren't a requirement in a kitchen. More and more, homeowners are switching some out with open shelves for a change of pace or doing away with them completely to give the kitchen a more open and airy feeling. On the other hand, wall cabinets are often a necessity to help store everything commonly found in a kitchen. And in today's open floor plans, wall cabinets can be strategically placed between the kitchen and living/dining area to create a strong visual boundary.

The standard wall cabinet is typically 12 in. deep and 30 in. high; if set at the preferred 18 in. above a standard 36-in.-high countertop, it won't reach all the way to a standard-height ceiling. Keep in mind, however, that a 12-in.-deep cabinet may not meet your needs. Oversize dinner plates and chargers may call for deeper wall cabinets, so be sure to take measurements before shopping for cabinets. Likewise, if an appliance—like a microwave—is planned for a wall cabinet, consider that most are more than 12 in. deep. Extra-deep wall cabinets—those measuring 15 in. or more—can be dropped down all the way to the countertop to make items more accessible. Just know that, as a result, you'll lose a good amount of countertop workspace.

Stacked cabinets to the right of this countertop feature a square transom cabinet on top. Two more extend over the window, the height of all making them the perfect place to showcase decorative items.

Simple styling doesn't necessarily mean the cabinets are less expensive. In fact, frameless cabinets like these are more painstaking to build and install, so they can take a bigger bite out of your budget.

•cabinetry basics

Before you set out shopping for cabinetry, it's important to keep a few measurements in mind. Standard wall cabinets are 30 in. high; if set at the suggested 15 in. to 18 in. above a standard 36-in. high countertop, they won't reach the ceiling. The space above the wall cabinets might be used for display, or the ceiling can be dropped to make a soffit. But today it's more popular to take cabinets all the way to the ceiling, either by installing wall cabinets higher or ordering taller cabinets. If you opt for taller cabinets, be sure doors will clear light fixtures and that there's sufficient space for trim between the doors and the ceiling.

Base cabinets are set on solid bases or on legs, which can be exposed or covered by trim. A common design detail is a toe space, a recessed area at the bottom of a base cabinet. Stock face-frame and many frameless manufactured cabinets have a 4-in.-high, 3-in.-deep toe space. European-style cabinets more often have tall toe spaces, measuring from 5 in. to 8 in. Besides making it more comfortable to work close to the countertop, the toe space can be designed to serve any number of purposes. It can be fitted with a pull-out drawer that holds a step stool, for instance, or provide a discreet place for an air register.

Mixing cabinet colors is a current trend, one that works particularly well in this kitchen. Gray base cabinetry is the perfect partner for stainless-steel appliances; white wall cabinets seem to all but fade away, making the kitchen appear larger.

ABOVE This face-frame cabinet—with graduated drawers, fanciful hardware, and carved legs—has a feminine look that's in keeping with a cottage-style kitchen like this. The addition of matching wall cabinetry creates the appearance of a hutch.

RIGHT The contrasting toe kick beneath these white contemporary cabinets—frameless units with overlay doors and drawers—gives them a floating appearance. The toe kick lends an element of continuity too, by matching the countertop.

STACKED AND TRANSOM WALL CABINETS

t he stacked, or two-level, wall cabinet has an elegance about it. The top cabinet, also referred to as a transom cabinet, can feature windows, which are often glazed and lit from within. And while the transom level is too high for everyday use, it's ideal for showcasing special pieces. Transom cabinets with solid doors are an option too; they're perfect for storing lesser-used items.

These stacked wall cabinets reach all the way to the ceiling, making the kitchen seem taller in the process. Mirrored door panels add to the spacious effect, bouncing light right back into the room.

LEFT Raised-panel doors and drawers are the norm in this wall of cabinetry. But the panels of two larger doors have been taken over for more practical purposes; for this busy family, there's a chalkboard as well as a magnet board.

BELOW Glass-fronted wall cabinets are ideal for displaying dinnerware. The back of this cabinet contrasts its blue-and-white tile surround, showcasing its pieces even more prominently.

Dark wood base cabinets with flat-slab doors and drawers set a contemporary tone in this kitchen. The lighter wall cabinetry follows the lead, the flat-slab doors are flanked by the same dark wood as the cabinets below.

UNIVERSAL DESIGN DETAILS FOR CABINETS

universal design is intended to make life easier for people of all ages and abilities. To make your cabinets more user friendly, consider these details:

- Use full-extension glides on drawers and pull-out shelves.

- Opt for accessories that pull out, rotate, or swing out, especially for corner cabinets.

- In lieu of traditional wall cabinets, opt for open shelving lowered a few inches. Or store the majority of your items in a pantry or in base cabinets.

- Make cabinet toe spaces deeper and taller, which will make it easier to negotiate with a wheelchair.

- Choose grab pulls instead of knobs, and lever handles for full-height and pantry doors.

- Provide a seated workspace somewhere in the kitchen.

- Use glass door panels that let you see what's stored at a glance.

Glass-fronted doors on both sides of this cabinet make it easy to see what's stored within (the hardware is on the opposite side). Better yet, it's easily accessible—even for someone in a wheelchair.

face-frame vs. frameless cabinets

●●● CABINETS START WITH THE BASIC BOX—referred to as the case, carcase, or carcass—which can be either face frame or frameless. A face-frame cabinet case gets its style and strength from a frame of horizontal rails and vertical stiles applied to the exposed front edges of the case. Doors mount to that frame, either fitting flush into the frame or overlaying all or part of it. Because it takes more time to construct components that must fit closely together, face-frame cabinets with inset doors and drawers are pricier than those with overlays. Partial-overlay face-frame cabinets are less expensive than full-overlay doors, simply because there's a wider gap between the doors and drawers.

A frameless cabinet—also known as a European cabinet—is a box with no face frame. Because there's no frame to add stability, the case itself must be built stronger than its face-frame counterpart; ¾-in.-thick sides make the sturdiest frameless case. From the outside, it's not always easy to distinguish face-frame cabinets from frameless; doors and drawers for both can be flush overlay. See "Discerning the Difference?" on the facing page to learn how to tell them apart.

All of the dark-stained cabinetry in this transitional kitchen is overlay, meaning the door and drawer fronts are not inset. Flat-slab drawers team up with frame-and-panel doors, and variegated tile makes them all stand out more prominently.

Contemporary to its very core, this kitchen features bright red lacquered frameless cabinets with full overlay (not inset) drawers. The cabinets' hardware echoes the stainless steel of the cooktop and oven as well as the smart-looking backsplash.

DISCERNING THE DIFFERENCE

THE CABINET CASE

- A **face-frame** cabinet can make it easier to fit cabinets into a space that isn't completely square and plumb because the frame can be scribed and cut to fit the space, while the case itself wouldn't need to be adjusted.
- A **face-frame** cabinet has a narrower opening than a **frameless** cabinet of the same width, so pull-out shelves and drawers will be narrower too.
- A **frameless** cabinet has no stile or rail in front of the contents, so it can be easier to pull out stored items; an exception is an especially wide cabinet, which may require a center post.
- A **face-frame** cabinet gets much of its strength from the frame, whereas a **frameless** cabinet depends on a stronger, thicker back and strong corner joints.

DOORS AND DRAWERS

- In **frameless** cabinets, doors and drawers usually overlay the case completely—

referred to as full overlay or flush overlay. **Frameless** cabinets rarely have inset doors.
- In **face-frame** cabinets, doors and drawers may overlay the frame completely, may be inset, or may overlay the frame partially (referred to as reveal overlay or half overlay).
- Inset doors, the standard in traditional-style cabinets, can require more precision in their construction and installation than overlay doors.

DOOR HARDWARE

- Concealed adjustable hinges are available for both **frameless** and **face-frame** cabinet doors. They commonly adjust in three directions and are easy to tweak over the life-time of a cabinet.
- Inset doors, used almost exclusively in **face-frame** cabinets, are typically hung with butt hinges, which require more precision to install than their adjustable counterparts.

These frameless cabinets, with full overlay drawers, are fitted with hardware that can handle their potentially hefty load. Graduated in size, the drawers accommodate a variety of cooking needs—from the smallest spices to large pots and pans.

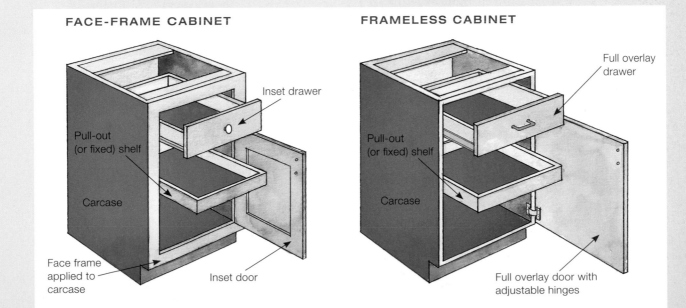

FACE-FRAME CABINET

- Inset drawer
- Pull-out (or fixed) shelf
- Carcase
- Face frame applied to carcase
- Inset door

FRAMELESS CABINET

- Full overlay drawer
- Pull-out (or fixed) shelf
- Carcase
- Full overlay door with adjustable hinges

doors and drawers

●●● WHEN MAKING DECISIONS ON DOOR and drawer faces, keep in mind that inset doors and drawers—which fit flush with a face frame—tend to be more costly than overlay doors because of the extra precision required. You'll find that hinges on inset cabinets are visible, with mortised butt hinges and leaf hinges being the most traditional styles.

Overlay doors and drawers affix to the surface of a face frame or the interior of a frameless case, while cup hinges make them easily adjustable. Full overlay doors and drawers, the standard on frameless cabinets but also used on face-frame types, all but touch each other. Thus they're more painstaking to build and install than reveal overlay doors and drawers, which are spaced farther apart. Reveal overlay doors and drawers—also called partial overlay—are used on face-frame cabinets.

Whether inset or overlay, doors and drawers are made in two basic types: frame and panel and flat slab. Frame-and-panel doors and drawer faces are more traditional in style, with a frame often made of solid wood and panels that are solid or veneered medium-density fiberboard (MDF). Panels themselves can be flat, beaded, beveled, perforated, carved wood, or glass. Flat-slab, or one-piece, doors and drawer faces are made from glued solid wood or MDF veneered with any number of materials, most commonly wood but also plastic laminate, metal, or even glass.

Set in face-frame cabinets, these raised-panel doors and drawers are perfectly suited for a traditional kitchen. Stained a medium brown, they all feature the same easy-to-grab pulls, their color picking up the black in the tile backsplash.

LEFT Think of stainless-steel cabinets and you may conjure up something hard-edged and cold. But this kitchen softens the look with marble and warm wood elements. Cabinetry goes all the way to the ceiling too, using every inch of space.

BELOW Their turquoise color takes these flat-slab doors and drawers from ordinary into the realm of extraordinary. While the hue gives this kitchen an up-to-the-minute look, brass hardware keeps it from going ultra-contemporary.

RIGHT If a cabinet's door swing can potentially be cumbersome—especially if the case is set up all the way to the ceiling—sliding doors can present a good solution. The back of this glass-front cabinet is finished in green-painted beadboard, contrasting the white tile backsplash below.

RIGHT Flat frame-and-panel drawers are a good fit for this built-in bench; their very appearance gives them a feeling of strength and support. Bin pulls are easy to grasp, important at a lower level like this.

BELOW Base cabinets in this kitchen feature flat-slab drawer fronts with inset hardware; meanwhile, wall cabinets have frame-and-panel doors with pulls, punctuated by tambour-door counterparts that reach all the way to the counter for an added dose of convenience.

BASE CABINETS: DRAWER FACE AND DOOR OPTIONS

the two basic categories of drawers and doors are frame and panel and flat slab. Some cabinet cases are shown in the drawings as frameless and some as face frame, but either category of doors and drawers can be used in either type of cabinet. Although door and drawer faces should be compatible, they don't need to be identical. Keep in mind that detailing on shallow drawers looks best if it's simpler than that on a door or wide drawer.

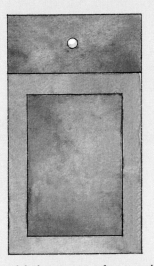

Flat-slab drawer over a frame-and-panel door with concealed hinges

A shallow drawer often looks less fussy with a flat-slab face rather than a face-frame, plus it pairs well with any kind of door.

Drawer in a beaded-edge frame over a beaded frame-and-raised-panel door with butt hinges

The drawer face echoes the beading detail on the door design but doesn't go so far as to repeat the raised panel.

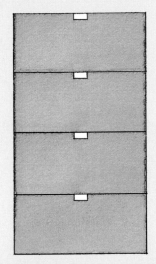

A stack of same-size flat-slab overlay drawers with finger pulls

The clean-lined overlay drawers have a contemporary look, enhanced by the streamlined hardware.

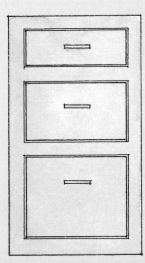

Graduated drawers in a beaded face-frame case with intermediate rails

Intermediate rails provide both strength and a traditional look. Beading the frame instead of the drawer also offers a simpler detail that will withstand the test of time.

Graduated drawers in a face-frame cabinet without intermediate rails

Eliminating the intermediate rails between drawers has a less traditional look but provides more cabinet capacity.

•drawer construction

Make no mistake: Drawers do some heavy lifting, so be sure that yours are up to the task. Because they could be supporting pots and pans, as well as stacks of dishes, look for drawer boxes built with 1/2-in. to 3/4-in. melamine, solid wood, or birch plywood. Shallow drawers may have side panels as thin as 1/2 in. Metal and plastic sides also have sufficient strength and have a certain streamlined look. Keep in mind that drawers that carry particularly heavy loads should have thick bottoms. The strongest, best-looking drawers have dovetailed corners, but corners that are doweled, screwed, or stapled are less expensive and—if built well—can do the job. For the most part, hardware is a matter of personal preference. But a wide drawer—one that measures 24 in. or more—requires two knobs, two short pulls, or one long pull.

Although any drawer wider than 24 in. should be fitted with either extra-long hardware or multiple hardware fixtures, this kitchen goes the extra mile. At the desk, a pull that spans nearly the entire width of the drawer adds to the dramatic impact.

ABOVE Providing storage for pots and pans, this storage door couldn't be handier. With one easy movement, the cook can grab the item of choice to use at the adjacent cooktop.

LEFT Located directly under the countertop where plates are set out for serving—and next to the warming oven too—an extra-strong drawer keeps dishes close at hand. Wooden peg dividers hold the dishes in place.

d rawers are operated by glides, also referred to as guides or slides. Full-extension glides allow access to the entire length of a drawer, a convenience that may well outweigh the extra expense, especially for big drawers that hold pots and pans. Quiet, self-closing glides are another feature you may want to spring for, especially if there are "enthusiastic" drawer and door closers in the house. If you don't like the look of side-mounted slides, consider undermounts, though they are more expensive than side mounted. Undermounts eat up a little space from the depth of the drawer but side-mounted glides shave a bit off the width.

A tall sliver of space in this kitchen is dedicated to pull-out shelves that offer a clear view of their contents. And the side-mounted glides keep everything corralled.

materials and finishes

●●● ALL CABINETS ARE NOT CREATED EQUAL. Most are made of wood—whether solid or veneered onto cabinet cases, doors, and drawers—and come in a wide variety of species and finishes. If you live in a moist climate, solid wood may not be your best bet; instead, consider wood veneered onto a more stable material, such as high-quality plywood. Quartersawn oak, cherry, Douglas fir, pine, hickory, chestnut, and maple are some of the best choices for traditional cabinetry, but they can adapt to modern styling too. Mahogany, bamboo, and zebrawood are typically reserved for contemporary cabinetry. Most wood cabinets are sprayed with catalyzed varnish although hand-applied finishes provide a true vintage look. Be aware, though, that hand-applied glazes and paints and high-gloss lacquer are the most costly finishes. Painted cabinets—especially those with glossy finishes—also show dings more easily than clear-finished wood cabinets, and may not be as easy to touch up. Door and drawer panel products (plywood or MDF) can be veneered with wood, rigid thermofoil (known as RTF, this plastic-face material is thermoformed to an engineered wood core such as fiberboard), metal, and 21st-century plastic laminate, while stainless-steel and coated-steel cabinets offer professional-quality shine.

more about...
CABINET CASE MATERIALS

When it comes to cabinets, beauty is more than skin deep; it's important to look beyond the facades of the doors and drawers to see what your cabinet cases are made of. There are mixed opinions as to what makes the best cabinet case. For years, the highest quality **wood** cabinet cases have been made from ¾-in. veneer-core plywood, which is stronger, lighter weight, and more moisture-resistant than medium-density fiberboard (**MDF**) or **particleboard**. On the other hand, some cabinetmakers prefer MDF over plywood for its dimensional stability and its smooth face that's ideal for applying veneers and other laminates, plus it's typically less expensive than veneer-core plywood. Finally, while there's no arguing that particleboard is the lowest-quality of case goods, it's also the least expensive—and the most commonly used in manufactured cabinets.

If your budget allows, choose plywood for cabinets where water could potentially cause damage. For dry locations, look to MDF or even particleboard, but also consider the plywood mashup combi-core, which retains a strong and light veneer plywood core but is sandwiched between layers of MDF to provide a smooth, stable surface.

FACING PAGE TOP Slab-style cabinets are often the first choice in contemporary kitchens; the unadorned face panels provide a sleek, streamlined look. Two distinct types of lacquer cabinetry distinguish the wall and base units here, both contributing to the soothing neutral scheme.

FACING PAGE BOTTOM LEFT The rich grain of this warm wood cabinetry becomes even more pronounced against the white subway-tile backsplash. To the right of the sink, carved-out drawer grips fall into the category of universal design; they're easy to grasp—but still handsome.

FACING PAGE BOTTOM RIGHT Clean-lined frame-and-panel cabinetry runs throughout this kitchen, its cream color adding an element of warmth. The cabinets' hardware is just as understated in style, making one a good companion for the other.

hardware

●●● IT MAY SEEM LIKE A SMALL PART OF THE decision-making process, but the right hardware can make a big impact on your kitchen's sense of style. Think of pairing cabinets with knobs, pulls, and hinges like fashion accessories; you can perfectly match your pieces or go for an eye-catching contrast. One approach might be to choose a single finish—polished nickel or oil-rubbed bronze, for instance—then vary pull sizes with those of the cabinet doors and drawers. Use wider pulls or two knobs for wide drawers and narrow pulls or a single knob for drawers that are narrow. Keep in mind, however, that finishes with the same name may not match exactly between hardware manufacturers; to be on the safe side, always compare samples in person. Then again, you may not want all of your hardware to match; mixing finishes on a wall of cabinetry can show off your one-of-a-kind style.

LEFT The world of hardware presents a multitude of options, among them metal, wood, and ceramic. But don't be afraid to have a little fun; these alphabet pulls give new meaning to kitchen organization.

ABOVE On this face-frame cabinet, a simple brass knob is all that's needed, and it won't visually conflict with the pieces stored behind the frame-and-glass-panel door.

KNOBS AND PULLS

When choosing knobs and pulls for doors and drawers, it's important to keep the size of one in proportion to the other. A 1¼-in. knob, for instance, is a good size for a standard-size drawer. A knob with a rose—the round plate at the base of the shaft—can keep things neater, simply because fingers are less likely to touch the drawer itself. By the same token, bin pulls have a cleaner look because they're pulled from the inside; on the downside, however, they are a little more difficult to clean than are knobs.

Drawers more than 24 in. wide typically require one long pull, or two pulls or knobs; if you opt for two, always use both to keep the drawer from eventually racking. In addition, knobs and pulls on drawers—which usually have a face attached to the drawer box—require longer screws than those for door hardware. Finally, you can forgo knobs and pulls altogether and opt instead for recessed pulls or invisible catches that open when you push on the doors or drawers.

The simplicity of these linear pulls complements the straightforward design of the cabinetry, allowing the rich wood grain to take the starring role.

add a fresh look with hardware

With a small investment, and even less time, new hardware can give your cabinetry a fresh new look. There are glass versions with vintage style, metal renditions that take on the appearance of twigs and leaves, even painted ceramic styles that can play up your kitchen's color scheme. In short, there are designs that reflect virtually any penchant or personal style.

Ceramic pulls in a bright yellow hue add a cheery touch to the sage-green cabinets—and the entire kitchen.

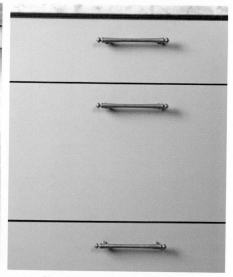

The brass pulls on these turquoise cabinets are right at home in the modern kitchen, but they'd be equally at ease in traditional quarters too.

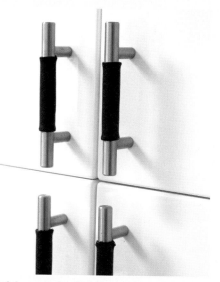

Stainless-steel pulls wrapped in leather give this cabinetry an undisputed contemporary attitude.

Quartersawn oak is typically thought of as traditional, but the more-contemporary hardware used on it here results in a transitional look.

Antiques stores and flea markets are good sources for vintage hardware like this, but you can also find plenty of new alternatives that look old.

Because these brass handles are easy to grab, they fall into the category of universal design—a plus for any age or ability.

more about...
HINGES

oncealed *adjustable hinges*, long the standard for frameless cabinets, are now available for inset doors in face-frame cabinets too. Adjustable hinges allow cabinet doors to be tweaked during installation—and even years later—sometimes permitting doors to swing open completely and out of traffic. Most cabinet doors require two hinges, but tall doors, such as those used for pantries, may require three or even more. Consider adjustable hinges with a built-in soft-closing feature if your family is prone to slamming doors.

Traditionally used for inset doors, *butt hinges* are either nonmortised (surface mounted) or mortised (set into the case). Installing mortised butt hinges requires extra time and precision but creates a smooth fit between the door and the frame. If cabinet hinges aren't self-closing, catches may be required. Catches range from invisible rare-earth magnets, which can be inserted into both door and stile or case to hold the door shut, to knobs that you physically turn to open. Latches, which swing up to open, look authentically old but take extra effort to use. As for a glass-door cabinet, a butt hinge or the olive-knuckle hinge (when closed, only the single hinge "knuckle" shows) are the best choices, simply because a concealed adjustable hinge would be more visible.

Depending on the cabinet, hinges can be mounted on the inside or outside. But under this sink, hinges are taken to an entirely new level. Custom wrought-iron versions end in intertwining leaves, a nod to the woodsy outdoor view.

LEFT The hinges on these wall cabinets allow the doors to lift vertically, making all of the contents within accessible. Plus the pneumatic system keeps a raised door in the same position until it's released.

ABOVE Hardware can be as simple and straightforward—or as sophisticated—as you like. This stainless-steel pull sets the bar high, as its sculptural form is a work of art in its own right.

cabinet accessories

● ● ● IN THE CASE OF CABINETRY, MORE ISN'T always better. Well-organized cabinetry can make a huge difference, allowing you to sort, store, and easily access your kitchen items in fewer cubic feet. Some accessories simply divide space while others are mechanical, sliding out, up, or down. And those like the familiar lazy Susan rotate. Cabinet accessories can be built in during the manufacturing process, or purchased as part of a stock or semistock cabinet package. Plus you'll find all kinds of after-market accessories online and in big-box stores. Consider built-in vertical slots for flat items such as trays and cutting boards. If you prefer to keep your stand mixer out of sight until baking time, an appliance garage is one option; those with lift-up, tilt-in, or swing doors are particularly good choices. But a spring-up shelf also allows you to store a mixer or other heavy appliance under the counter until you need it, while pull-out shelves can handle small appliances too.

Many cooks like to have a TV in the kitchen, though finding just the right location for it can be a challenge. Here, the television pulls out of a custom cabinet; when not in use, it slides back into the adjacent pantry.

A charging port is one of today's most-requested kitchen amenities. This single drawer under the microwave is custom-fitted for just that.

more about...
CORNER ACCESSORIES

blind cabinet corners can be a challenge, but that doesn't mean there aren't multiple solutions. Look for a lazy Susan, for instance; one without a center post offers more flexible storage while one with wire shelves has better visibility. You'll also find swing-out and pull-out racks that allow full access but keep in mind that their construction is more complex; the more moving parts, the more expensive they will be. Wall cabinets have corners too, but due to their shallow depth and eye level height, they aren't as difficult to access. Finally, you might opt for open shelving; it's completely accessible and can make a kitchen seem more spacious.

Taking full advantage of what could have been a hard-to-access corner, shelves swing out from behind a standard cabinet door. Short side rails ensure that items don't fall out when moved back and forth.

This set of corner drawers allows owners to find exactly what they're looking for by opening one at a time.

more about...
TRASH AND COMPOST

well-organized kitchen includes cabinets outfitted for trash, compost, and recycling. What type of containers you choose and where you locate them depends primarily on your cooking habits. Contrary to what most people think, the cabinet under the sink is not the best place to put trash and recycling. Instead, locate pull-out garbage bins near food-prep areas, to the right or left of the wash-up sink—or both of those work zones. A pedal-operated trash cabinet allows the cook to dump trimmings without ever touching the handle with dirty hands. Another option is a trash bin attached to a door panel operated by a touch latch or, more simply, hooked open with your foot. Compost bins can be mounted under a countertop hole, as a pull-out or even a built-in drawer. But compost bins must be easy to remove, clean, and replace daily. A simple bin on the countertop may take up less precious storage space—and you won't forget to empty it.

ABOVE RIGHT A vast array of accessories are available to make your kitchen its most efficient. And, sometimes, it's the smallest detail that can provide the greatest convenience. This built-in paper towel holder is perfectly placed next to the sink.

RIGHT Shelves that pull out and even spring up are an added convenience in any kitchen; small appliances stored there can be used without ever being moved from the shelves. But don't neglect an important detail: Be sure there's a nearby electrical outlet.

An appliance garage in this kitchen repeats the angle of the counter itself, providing a convenient place for canisters as well as a coffee maker and the proper accouterments.

drawers versus pull-out shelves

There was a time when fixed shelves were the only option in base cabinets. But pull-out shelves are now an alternative, making it easier to see cabinet contents. And, with the advent of heavy-duty glide hardware, even pots and pans once hung on hooks or stashed on higher shelves can be conveniently stored in base cabinets.

So what's best for you? All drawers or a combination of drawers and pull-out shelves? Pull-out shelves have low sides and fronts that allow a quick inventory of their contents. The shelves can usually be adjusted to suit the containers you want to store but, on the other hand—because pull-out shelf walls aren't as high as those of a drawer—items can fall out; a drawer is better at corralling its contents. Another advantage of a drawer is that it takes just one motion to see what's inside; with a pull-out shelf, you first have to open a cabinet door and then tug on the shelf. (There are base cabinets, however, that feature a stack of pull-out shelves attached directly to the cabinet door panel that glides straight out with one motion.) Finally, you may want to consider cost: An all-drawer base cabinet will be more expensive than one with a drawer on top and a door concealing pull-out shelves on the bottom.

Clean-lined cabinetry in this modern kitchen was designed to meet the owners' every need. Next to the refrigerator, a pull-out drawer holds a well-stocked bar while an adjacent tall cabinet keeps all manner of cleaning materials close at hand.

LEFT Corner-turning pull-out shelves allow the owner to access everything stashed in this cabinet. And with the slim pull-out shelf at the top, not an inch of space was wasted, either.

ABOVE Platters are easily accessible in this base cabinet drawer. Best of all, the partitions can be moved at a moment's notice to suit ever-changing needs.

BELOW Kitchen utensils don't need to clutter countertops or drawers. This pull-out cabinet accommodates canisters that keep spoons, whisks, and spatulas close to the stove.

ABOVE Double-decker storage accommodates oils and vinegars in this pull-out cabinet. Low rails allow easy access on one side while taller glides on the other keep items in place.

•cabinet sources

Cabinets' sources run the gamut and, in fact, your components are likely to come from various places. Even custom cabinetmakers may shop out components to specialized sources and then assemble them in their own shops. Stock and semicustom cabinets increasingly come from one of the many cabinet manufacturers that purchase cabinet parts from companies that specialize in doors, drawers, or cases. And, in fact, you can mix and match yourself. You might opt for custom or semicustom cabinets for high visibility locations, such as the island, and use stock or DIY cabinets for perimeter locations. No matter what route you take, carefully study any plans or shop drawings you have for specifications, and then make a detailed shopping list, right down to the last piece of hardware.

more about...
CUSTOM CABINETS

ontrary to popular belief, custom cabinets—those crafted in a cabinetmaker's shop—aren't necessarily the most expensive. They can be if their fabrication takes longer than semicustom cabinets. But a cabinetmaker may not be building your cabinets from scratch; instead, he or she may be combining components from several specialized sources with shop-built cases. If those components are made well, this approach to cabinetmaking can result in both a shorter lead time and a better product. And it may be a less-expensive alternative to higher-end semicustom cabinetry, so do check out local cabinet shops. Be sure, though, to always ask a cabinetmaker for references, and take time to see the referenced cabinetry in person.

TOP Taking convenience one step further, this coffee machine is flanked by pull-out doors that keep cups at the ready. Short side rails on one side keep them readily accessible while solid panels on the other keep them in place.

ABOVE As if a convenient coffee spot weren't enough, this cabinetry is fitted to serve up morning toast too. The right side of this drawer holds a four-slice toaster (as well as a built-in electrical outlet); bread is stored beneath the sliding board on the left.

Floor-to-ceiling custom cabinetry keeps all manner of kitchen essentials close at hand. That includes a coffee machine, essential to these owners' morning routine. Situated approximately at eye-level height, it couldn't be more convenient.

Many of today's stock and semicustom cabinets can look similar to their custom counterparts, especially when it comes to contemporary styles like this. If you can plan your kitchen around standard cabinet sizes, you can often find stock units; otherwise, semicustom may be your best bet.

more about...
STOCK AND SEMICUSTOM CABINETS

Stock cabinets can be purchased right off the shelf. More often, though, they're ordered from a big-box store, home center, or lumberyard, or through a kitchen products dealer, designer, or contractor. And installation is generally available for an additional fee. Stock cabinets are typically built in standard-size components in 3-in. increments, but if a run of cabinets isn't quite as wide as you need, there are stock filler pieces that can span the gaps. Or, to create a more custom look, you can cover gaps, embellish corners—even top wall cabinets with cornices—with pieces purchased from decorative molding suppliers. Available in a wide array of styles and sizes, colors and finishes, stock cabinets typically run about half the cost of semicustom and custom cabinets.

Semicustom cabinets are also manufactured (as opposed to shopmade) but they are made to order for a specific project and from a wider range of styles, finishes, hardware, accessories, sizes, and configurations than are stock cabinets. Cabinets can also be built as larger assemblies rather than simply case by case. Semicustom cabinetry tends to be higher quality and higher priced than stock cabinets, sometimes by a considerable amount.

ABOVE Both semicustom and custom cabinets offer flatware drawers fitted with handsome wood dividers. This one takes a two-tier approach; the top tier can slide back and forth, depending on what's needed at the moment.

ABOVE What first appears to be twin hutches in this kitchen is, in fact, one long run of cabinetry with matching wall cabinets above. The wall units—stretching all the way to the ceiling—feature mullioned doors that replicate the look of the windows.

more about...
DO-IT-YOURSELF CABINETS

ⓘ f there's a handyman in the house, DIY cabinetry may fill the bill. Knockdown (KD) and ready-to-assemble (RTA) cabinets are made up of factory-manufactured components that are shipped with all parts, fasteners, and instructions—no special power tools are required. You will find both KD and RTA sources online. Keep in mind, however, that buying your cabinets off the shelf will cost less than if the cabinets have to be shipped.

All cabinetry offers a wide range of accessories, built right in before cabinets arrive at your door. But there are plenty of after-market options as well, like this one that keeps the cutting board close to where it's used.

more about...
COMPARING COSTS

p ricing cabinetry can be a complex task, but the first thing to know is this: Simple doesn't necessarily equate to less expensive. A high-quality, stain-grade solid-wood frame-and-flat-panel door will typically cost more than a stain-grade raised-panel MDF door, even with beading and other detailing. And the less finishing required, the more economical the cabinets will be. A straight run of cabinets that fits between two walls, for instance—so there's no need for end panels—will be less costly than the same length of island cabinetry that is visible on all sides. Refacing your existing kitchen cabinets with new doors and drawer fronts is an option as well, but doesn't always cost less than buying new cabinets. Plus it's a valid option only if your cabinet cases are in good shape and you're happy with your present cabinet configuration.

Mixing cabinet styles can reveal your inner creativity, and maybe save a few dollars too. If you plan to use stock cabinets and can't find enough of one, complement it with another. The result could be an eye-catching focal point like the one in this contemporary kitchen.

open shelves and pantries

● ● ●

WHILE MOST KITCHEN GEAR IS STASHED BEHIND CABINETRY DOORS or in drawers, there's much to be said about open shelving. Whether it's within the confines of the kitchen proper or tucked into an adjacent space, open shelving can make the room seem more spacious. In addition, their simple, straightforward design makes open shelves an economical substitute for conventional wall cabinets.

Open shelves also have the advantage of being easily accessible. Neat rows of spice jars within reach of the cooktop will likely bring out one's inner master chef. Likewise, plates stacked on an open shelf will speed up both the getting-out and putting-away aspects of mealtime. Your best bets for open shelves will be any frequently used items. As if spaciousness, cost-effectiveness, and convenience weren't enough to make open shelves attractive, there is one more advantage: They're incentive to keep things tidy.

On the other hand, what if you prefer to keep oft-used items out of sight but still conveniently close? A pantry can be the perfect solution, whether behind the doors and drawers of kitchen cabinetry or a space unto itself, surrounded by three walls and a door. The latter provides easy access to items without the inevitable dust and grease that can accumulate in a kitchen and can be as large or small as you like. And a butler's pantry—typically a transitional space between the kitchen and dining room—can be fitted with a mix of closed storage and open shelves. If you do, however, prefer to keep your pantry items within the kitchen itself, you'll find plenty of cabinets outfitted to meet your specific needs.

Simple wood shelves are perfectly placed in this kitchen. Not only are the dishes they hold easily accessible for mealtime but, because the shelves are directly above the sink and dishwasher, the putting-away process is a breeze too.

open shelves

● ● ● WHEN IT COMES TO SIZING UP SHELVES the general rule is this: There are no rules. Open shelves can go anywhere and be any size at all. Near the prep area, narrow shelves can accommodate spices and cooking oils, even wooden spoons and other cooking utensils. Deeper shelves can hold larger—and lesser used—serving pieces, as well as hefty cookbooks. Recessed shelves are an option too, though they should be tucked into interior walls where insulation is not a concern. And before cutting into existing walls, always make exploratory holes to determine if any utilities are running in the wall.

While shelves can be any size, those positioned over countertops must be narrow enough to allow you to still work comfortably. For instance, over-the-counter shelves that are longer than 15 in. to 18 in. should be no deeper than 12 in. and the counters below should still have sufficient light. Like wall cabinets, the underside of an open shelf can be fitted with task lighting, with the front trimmed to conceal the fixture.

ABOVE Open shelves showcase a collection of delicate pottery in this casually contemporary kitchen. And because the black and white pieces are tucked into a niche, they're safely out of harm's way.

LEFT Set against herringbone-patterned ceramic tile panels, open and airy wall shelves on either side of the range hood echo its graceful, swooping lines. But it's as much about function as fashion here; everyday dinnerware is strategically placed on the bottom shelves, where it's easiest to reach.

A single, corner-turning shelf connects cabinetry in this kitchen, continuing the line of the wall cabinet's bottom edge. The horizontally placed wood planks above the shelf contrast their white-painted vertical counterparts below, giving both more prominence in the process.

more about...
STORAGE TIPS

a s a rule of thumb for storing or displaying things that you use frequently, the shelf should be just slightly deeper than the objects themselves. That way, it's less likely that you'll place more items along the shelf's front edge. If your home is fitted with deep shelves, though, there are some strategic solutions. First, reserve deep shelves for decorative objects, items that you won't need to retrieve on a regular basis. Or, along the back of the shelf, set canisters filled with kitchen staples such as flour and sugar, keeping in mind that rectangular containers are better than round; they make the most of your space. In front of the containers, set long, narrow—and lightweight—bins or baskets to corral small like items such as food processor attachments. This kind of a stair-stepped approach allows you to see everything at a glance for easier retrieval.

gallery

special-purpose storage

The beauty of custom cabinetry is that you can have it crafted to meet your specific needs—from an entire library of cookbooks to your favorite bottles of wine.

Open shelves in this kitchen island come in the form of pullouts, keeping pots and pans close at hand and—when not in use—conveniently out of the way.

A sliver of space in this kitchen is just wide enough for dedicated wine storage. If possible, this kind of storage should be located on a cooler side of the house—the north or the east.

The back side of a custom cabinet located between the kitchen and dining area provides a fitting place to showcase the owner's collection of china.

Open shelves at the end of this bank of cabinets keep a stash of cookbooks close at hand yet out of the way of anyone working in the kitchen proper.

Custom cabinetry in this cottage-style kitchen incorporates open shelving that artfully displays a variety of cookbooks and collectibles. Because they're backed by a patterned wallpaper, the crisp white shelves appear more prominent.

In this transitional kitchen, exposed shelves on either side of the room's single window keep things open and airy. Wall-hung cabinets with doors would have not only made the room seem smaller but also created a tunnellike view to the window.

Light strips tucked behind the open shelves in this kitchen brighten the entire area, making individual pieces easier to see in the process.

ABOVE Open shelves in this bar keep glassware neatly organized by type. Their staggered placement is visually pleasing but practical too: There's less likelihood of knocking down one glass while reaching for another.

LEFT Just as clean-lined and streamlined as the rest of this kitchen, these open shelves accommodate everything needed to set the nearby table. Their neutral hue blends into the background as well, adding to the room's spacious feeling.

•shelf materials

Selecting the best shelf material for your kitchen comes down, in large part, to aesthetics. Solid-wood and panel products can take either a traditional or contemporary tack, while glass shelves are most often used in contemporary spaces. But if glass is your material of choice, keep this in mind: Most shelf glass has a green tint. If you prefer a more colorless glass, look for a low-iron variety. There are other options, as well. Covered-wire shelves are a budget-friendly choice while restaurant-quality wire shelving can re-create the gleam of a professional kitchen.

But selecting shelf materials is about more than just looks; a shelf's strength and span are also deciding factors. Solid wood is relatively strong, but it can warp. Plus it expands and contracts with changes in humidity. Veneered plywood is not only more stable than solid wood, but can also pass for solid wood if its edges are covered with a glue-on or iron-on edging or edge-band (which also increases the strength of the shelf). Although MDF and particleboard can't span as far as solid wood or plywood shelves of the same thickness and depth, they're certainly serviceable if their supports are close enough together to prevent sagging.

In a kitchen where every inch of storage space counts, ingenuity comes to the rescue. Here, a glass shelf spans the width of two windows, providing a place for everyday items while not interrupting the natural light that floods the room.

The beauty of these open shelves lies in their simplicity. Their stainless-steel surface echoes that of the nearby sink, while adding an element of easy-to-clean practicality.

A single, white-painted wood shelf is the perfect place for everyday glassware, placed just a step or two from the kitchen sink.

MAKE SHELVES STRONGER

*i*t's essential that any shelf be strong enough to carry its potential load. Here's how you can strengthen a shelf:

- Keep spans short. An increase in span of just 25% results in twice as much deflection.
- Add intermediate shelf supports.
- Opt for fixed shelves; because they're stronger than adjustable shelves, they can have longer spans. Plus there's no need to drill intermittent holes on each side of the cabinet.
- To increase the load a shelf can support and the distance it can span between brackets, add a cleat—a narrow board or molding—continuously below the shelf and against the wall.
- To increase the visual heft of a shelf and make it more rigid, apply a wood edge-band (a 1½-in. edge-band is common) to the front edge.
- Double the thickness of a shelf by attaching two boards to one another, then finish the front edge of the double-thickness shelf with an edge-band that covers the joint.
- Build a torsion box, a thick shelf that is similar to a hollow-core door, with a honeycomb structure or plywood strips faced with two plywood skins.

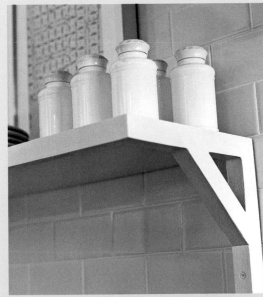

Even the simplest bracket can increase the load that a shelf can carry. This one resonates with the same understated tone as the rest of the kitchen.

pantries

●●● A PANTRY CAN TAKE ON MANY FORMS. A cabinet pantry can be crafted to match the rest of the kitchen's cabinetry while a reach-in pantry—the size of a single or double closet—keeps essentials nearby but at the kitchen's perimeter. A pantry can even be the size of a small room; walk-in and butler's pantries are built right into the house structure. Each type has its advantages. A cabinet pantry is typically within the work triangle while a reach-in pantry is removed from the work triangle but has the same benefit of displaying its contents by opening a single door. Meanwhile, both the walk-in and butler's pantries are spacious enough to accommodate dinnerware, food-prep space, and even secondary appliances.

Any pantry will be handiest if it's close to where you need it most. Locate a spice pantry adjacent to the food-prep space, for instance, and a dish pantry between the serving area and the dishwasher. As for built-in pantry closets, there is one more consideration; if you have a choice, locate them on cool exterior walls—on the north or east side of the house.

A pocket door allows you to take advantage of every square inch of a pantry. This one, with its frosted glass, is see-through to a degree; a solid door would have made the kitchen seem smaller.

more about...
CABINET PANTRIES

abinet-style pantries come in a wide variety of configurations. They can blend quietly into the rest of your kitchen's cabinetry, measuring the same height and depth. Or they can take on the appearance of a china cabinet, with the top cabinet stepped back from a deeper base. If you have no more than a sliver of space, a narrow rollout unit is another solution. With closely spaced fixed shelves behind the cabinet door, this type of pantry offers quick access to everything from spices to dishwashing essentials. As with all custom cabinetry, though, the more complex the accessories, the higher the price. One way to cut costs is to start with simple, straightforward cabinets, then customize them with aftermarket dividers and other accessories.

This cabinet pantry sets itself apart from the rest of the room's storage with its woven metal doors. In addition to being decorative, they allow you to see at a glance what's inside.

A custom combination of cabinet components gives this pantry the look of a traditional china cupboard. There is nothing traditional, though, about the citrus orange color, sure to enliven any kitchen.

more about...
WALK-IN AND
REACH-IN PANTRIES

While walk-in and reach-in pantries have their differences, there are similarities too. Both, for instance, should have a variety of shelf depths. Shallow shelves (4 in. to 12 in. deep) high on the wall will allow you to see and store cans, jars, and bottles. Deeper 18-in. to 20-in. shelves for bulky items are best placed lower down, perhaps under a work counter. Adjustable shelves or freestanding shelving kits will make it easy to change the configuration over the years, but if you're set on a certain configuration fixed shelves can be more stable. Solid-wood shelving is one fixed option but the covered-wire type offers better visibility and ventilation. Whatever type of shelving you choose, baskets work well for corralling small items and are easy to take out and put back. If space allows, a countertop can provide a place to store and use small appliances or to cool just-baked cookies.

In a walk-in pantry, it's best not to cover all of the wall space with shelves; leave some room for hooks to hang aprons, a broom or vacuum, maybe even a message board. You may want to locate recycling bins in a larger walk-in pantry, especially if it's near the back door. Although standard doors are suitable for walk-in pantries, the door width of a reach-in pantry requires more consideration. If the reach-in pantry is shallow but wide, two doors are ideal; one wide door will swing out too far and a single standard door won't allow easy access. If space is tight, a pocket door can be a good alternative.

ABOVE RIGHT Floor-to-ceiling shelves provide more than ample storage in this walk-in pantry. The bonus, however, lies in the sink—and the extra prep space.

RIGHT Double doors that look like old-fashioned screens allow for easy access to this reach-in pantry. This type of swinging door is a good choice, as it closes entirely on its own.

ABOVE A double-door cabinet pantry is conveniently located within the kitchen work triangle, making it easy to grab the items inside. The well-lit interior makes it easier still.

LEFT Some of the most efficient cabinet pantries use door backs, in order to squeeze in as much easy-to-reach storage as possible. This one has the advantage of being extra-tall too.

TOP RIGHT This walk-in pantry features the best of two worlds. The open shelves inside make everything easily accessible while the glass door keeps the kitchen's grime at bay.

BOTTOM RIGHT A roll-out pantry specifically for spices is conveniently placed next to the range, ready for the cook to add a dash of this or a pinch of that at a moment's notice.

BELOW In a space where there's simply no room for a door swing, a roll-out cabinet can be the best solution. This one is especially efficient; it even extends past the edge of the kitchen floor.

Much more than a utilitarian element, this walk-in pantry—its cherry red facade punctuated by stainless-steel doors—is the focal point of this kitchen. The swinging doors make it easy to get in and out too.

more about...
LIGHTING A PANTRY

lighting a pantry is about more than illuminating the items within. Here, the heat factor comes into play. A fluorescent ceiling fixture just inside the door will stay cool and shed plenty of light on stored items, a charging station for personal electronics, and/or a countertop for small appliances. (Be sure to include the necessary receptacles after checking local codes for any special requirements.) Finally, consider a door-operated switch or motion detector so you don't forget to turn off the light.

BELOW A barn door–style entrance makes coming and going easy in this walk-in pantry. And there's no need for the shelves inside to be fancy; crafted of natural wood, they're all part of the country charm.

ABOVE This cabinet pantry, distinguished by its black color and decorative door panels, features shallow shelves on one side—perfect for spices and small canned goods—and a roll-out unit on another that fits neatly behind them.

more about...
THE BUTLER'S PANTRY

nlike the everyday pantry—hidden behind closed doors—the butler's pantry is typically a passageway between the kitchen and dining room, where cabinets prominently display dishes and glassware. It can be fitted with the same cabinetry found in the kitchen, have the same level of formality as the dining room, or exude an ambiance somewhere between. A butler's pantry requires a countertop, handy as a secondary food-prep space or as a buffet. And it's often home to a small sink as well as secondary appliances such as dishwashers, warming ovens, and refrigerators.

A wine aficionado's dream, this butler's pantry features adjustable, sized-to-fit shelves behind narrow doors for room-temperature bottles and a pair of refrigerators for those that need to be chilled.

countertops, backsplashes, and sinks

● ● ●

THERE'S NO DENYING THAT COUNTERTOPS TAKE THE BRUNT OF DAILY food prep. Still, given the fact that they're major players in the kitchen, we want them to look fabulous. The ideal countertop has it all: It's nonporous, nonstaining, heatproof, durable, easy to clean, scratch-resistant, and good looking. Oh, and inexpensive too. In reality, you'll most likely need to compromise here and there to find the countertop that's closest to ideal for your kitchen.

The perfect backsplash depends, a great deal, on where it will be placed. If it backs a food-prep area or sink, a backsplash must be stain- and/or water-resistant. Likewise, if it's behind a cooktop, a backsplash must hold up against a certain amount of heat. But if it's not adjacent to a workspace, a backsplash can beautifully showcase materials that wouldn't meet your countertop durability needs.

There's no need to pick just one countertop and/or backsplash, either. In fact, countertops and backsplashes can be mixed and matched to suit different kitchen tasks. A marble counter provides a cool, hard surface for rolling out dough while stainless-steel makes a sanitary, heatproof prep zone. And a ceramic tile backsplash is a good, hardworking choice for cooking or food-prep areas.

Good looks and performance are a must when it comes to sinks and faucets too. And don't forget about placement either. A lot of time is spent standing at a sink, so it needs to be comfortable for both your height and your work habits.

This single-bowl stainless-steel sink is both wide and deep, plenty big enough to accommodate cookie sheets and roasting pans. While it's hardworking, it's also good looking, complementing the marble countertops and white subway tile backsplash.

countertops and backsplashes

● ● ● THE IDEAL COUNTERTOP AND BACKSPLASH for your kitchen depends on your personal habits and expectations, so give each plenty of thought before making a purchase. A stone countertop with an irregular texture might be beautiful as a backsplash, but its rough surface might not be ideal behind an active cooktop; it's tough to clean the nooks and crannies, even if the stone has been sealed. Glossy surfaces have their challenges too; they show fingerprints and scratches more prominently. (If you don't want to give up the glamour of a certain material, simply make cutting boards mandatory.) Also be aware that a glossy backsplash or countertop will reflect undercabinet lighting as well as the undercabinet surface.

Prioritize your list of must-haves before shopping for countertops and backsplashes, then make a point of seeing the materials in person before making a purchase. Touch them. Run your hands across them. It might surprise you that countertops and backsplashes will be the most emotionally charged decisions you will make, so be sure to take your time. The reward will be surfaces that you will undoubtedly love.

Various shades of brown in this kitchen—in the cabinetry, the countertops, and the island—are all echoed in this tile backsplash. But the selection was based on more than aesthetic value; the backsplash stands up well to the heat of the cooktop.

ABOVE Sleek contemporary style is the order of the day in this kitchen, where marble countertops blend quietly into all-white cabinetry, a stainless-steel sink and faucet echo the finishes of the room's major appliances, and soft blue subway tiles lend just the right touch of color.

LEFT A beadboard backsplash may not be a good choice for a heavy-duty cooking zone but it's perfectly suitable in a less-active kitchen zone such as this bar area, where it's teamed with a handsome black granite countertop.

A variety of textures keeps things visually interesting in this neutral-themed kitchen. The countertops are made of hardworking CaesarStone®, while the eating bar features shimmering back-painted glass. Even the backsplash sports hand-crafted glass tile, complementing the matte-finished cabinets.

more about...
SIZING UP COUNTERTOPS

ⓘ t's perhaps safe to say that nobody has ever claimed to have too much counter space. So be sure to allot plenty in your kitchen. Most appliances require a 15-in. landing space on one or both sides, while each cook needs an uninterrupted 36-in.-wide space for food preparation. Likewise, height is important to consider. While 36-in.-high counters are standard, you may prefer some countertops at different heights. For most kitchen tasks, a comfortable height is 4 in. to 6 in. below the bent elbow, but some tasks—such as kneading dough and rolling pastry— are more comfortable on a lower surface.

ABOVE The warm wood cabinetry of this kitchen is beautifully balanced by the cooler tones of the granite countertops and the backsplash of tile and stainless steel. The latter, used behind the range, visually connects the appliance with the hood above it.

TOP Quartz countertops like these are a good choice for a kitchen; they can have the natural look and feel of granite, marble, and other quarried stones but feature superior strength and durability. A graphic backsplash is created with two tile colors, complementing the quartz that reappears in the form of windowsills.

ABOVE Light blue cabinets complement the glass tile backsplash, while honed black granite perimeter counters create both contrast and durable work surfaces. The island, on the other hand, is topped with maple, another hard-as-rock surface.

more about...
BACKSPLASH ALTERNATIVES

t he ideal backsplash fills the entire space between the countertop and the bottom of the wall cabinet, providing complete stain and water resistance; stone and tile are two of the most popular options. But if that's not possible, there are other solutions. A 4-in. plastic laminate cove backsplash is certainly adequate, but it can be made even better by using easy-to-clean satin or glossy paint—or even water-resistant wallpaper— above it. Likewise, a 6-in. to 12-in. decorative tile border or a 4-in. to 8-in. painted or stained wood molding can be topped off with paint or wallpaper. The bottom line is this: There are handsome, hardworking backsplashes to be had to suit every style and budget.

•countertop and backsplash materials

Given today's plethora of countertop and backsplash options, deciding which goes with what can be no small chore. It's smart to borrow—or even purchase—the largest samples available and live with them a while. Do the backsplash and countertop complement each other or clash?

Then there's the matter of durability, not to mention maintenance and, of course, cost. Regarding cost, be sure to factor in installation; some countertop and backsplash materials are DIY friendly while others need to be installed by licensed fabricators. If you want to go the do-it-yourself route, look at tile, wood, plastic laminate, and composite paper, as they can be worked on-site. Most other materials are prepared off-site, with small adjustments and cutouts handled on the job by experienced craftspeople; certain materials—such as solid surfacing and engineered stone—require a

manufacturer-certified installer. Finally, the design of your countertop will have a big impact on your budget. Consider such factors as the breadth and width of countertops, seam locations, and edge profiles as well as sink and faucet cutouts.

If an environmentally friendly material is important to you, understand that selection can be a complex issue. Ask yourself: Where do the materials come from? How are they made? Are they safe for your household? Will they stand up to use? Many factors go into determining whether a material is green, including transportation, content and origin of raw materials, manufacturing processes, and renewability. Stone, for instance, may be quarried close to you, but is it finished locally or is it done overseas? Can backsplash and countertop materials be recycled?

The island top in this kitchen is made of 2-in.-thick maple, oiled to give it a subtle contrast to the perimeter countertops and backsplash. Though they look like soapstone, they're actually schist, with a rich gray color and slight graining throughout.

ABOVE Color blocking makes this kitchen a visual masterpiece, starting with the two-tone cabinetry. The countertops follow suit, with honed granite and blue quartz, both predominantly used. Behind the cooktop, even a stainless-steel backsplash gets into the act.

LEFT Quartzite counters like this have a lot going for them. Formed when sandstone and quartz combine, the natural stone has a high resistance to heat and stains, plus it's durable and comes in a wide range of colors. This particular countertop is complemented by an iridescent glass backsplash that pulls out the stone's lighter tones.

SOLID WOOD AND BAMBOO

Wood makes a serviceable and beautiful countertop; it's warm in tone, soft to the touch, and easy on dishes. Wood can survive some heat too, although it can get scorched or stained by a hot or wet cast-iron pan. Just know this: Drying up spills immediately is essential to maintain a wood countertop.

Any species can make a decorative countertop, but strong woods make the best butcher-block countertops, with maple—and, more recently, end-grain bamboo—the standards. Both end-grain and edge-grain butcher-block make excellent cutting surfaces; face-grain wood, on the other hand, works well in serving or dining areas. Work-surface wood countertops are typically unsealed, though they are usually oiled with periodic rubdowns of mineral, tung, or linseed oil. Wood that won't be worked on directly can be sealed with polyurethane to protect it from moisture, but it should be finished on all sides (before installation) to prevent warping. If you're in search of an environmentally friendly wood, look for certification by the Forest Stewardship Council® (FSC).

Bamboo is technically a grass, but it's harder than most wood species and it matures much more quickly; it's ready to harvest in five years and grows back easily. That said, a considerable amount of adhesive is required to laminate bamboo strands together, so look for low- or no-volatile organic compound (VOC) glues. It should be treated like wood, with an oil applied to work surfaces or polyurethane applied to all sides

When planning a kitchen, incorporate countertops that are best suited to your everyday needs. This end-grain butcher block is perfect for chopping and food prep while the adjacent marble is ideal for kneading and rolling out dough.

FACING PAGE TOP LEFT Tiles that have the appearance of wood offer the best of two worlds; they're durable but offer the warmth of wood. The dark tiles in this kitchen make a strong statement between the lighter countertop and the wall-hung shelves.

FACING PAGE BOTTOM Black marble countertops and white subway-tiled walls are the epitome of understated elegance in this kitchen, allowing the focus to be on the eating bar, created with artistic-looking thick-cut wood. The irregular edges are all part of the charm.

BELOW Using more than one material for your countertops allows you to specify certain areas for specific tasks. The cold marble used around the perimeter of this room is good for food prep in general but even better for kneading and rolling out dough. The maple-topped island, meanwhile, doubles as an eating area and a sturdy chopping block.

ABOVE Mirrored tiles provide all the durability that's needed behind the cooktop in this kitchen, with a touch of sparkle for good measure. This material is a particularly good choice in small spaces, as it visually expands a room's dimensions.

ABOVE The stainless-steel backsplash behind this cooktop has a diamond pattern that—in addition to providing a tough, heat-resistant element—bounces light back into the kitchen.

RIGHT A honed black granite countertop subtly underscores a metal mosaic tile backsplash, the miniature squares echoing the pattern of the mullioned windows above. What's more, the black grout creates a tie to the countertop.

Stainless steel is far and away the most popular of metal countertop materials. It stands up to heat and water like no other surface, yet it's cool enough for rolling out pie dough. Plus it's durable and easy to keep clean. Even better, stainless steel can be formed with an integral sink or backsplash, making it completely watertight. But a word to the wise: There's no way to avoid scratches, so go for brushed surfaces that better disguise fingerprints and scratches.

A 16-gauge stainless-steel countertop will suit most kitchens (the lower the gauge number, the thicker the steel), formed around or supported by wood or MDF to add strength and mute sound. When budgeting for stainless, factor length into the price; 10 ft. is the cutoff before the price per square foot goes up. Some homeowners prefer the modified marine edge, a rounded lip that keeps smaller spills on the countertop, while others like how the square profile makes it easier to sweep chopped food into a pot. A bullnose edge is best for countertops that won't see water, as the half-round profile will allow dripping onto the cabinets below.

Still, other metals have their devotees. **Copper** is beautiful and will develop a patina, either naturally or with the application of chemicals or heat. Copper is soft, however, shows scratches, and is expensive. **Zinc** is softer than stainless steel and more moderately priced. But zinc can't be scrubbed with abrasive cleaner, and seams can show due to the material's variable color. Be wary too of putting hot cast-iron pans on zinc or copper as discoloration can occur. **Pewter** is extremely expensive and easy to scratch, but it adds a European-look to your kitchen. **Bronze** oxidizes like copper but to a lesser degree; it's stronger than copper and somewhat more expensive.

Proving once and for all that the kitchen is much more than a practical place, this kitchen turns what could have been a mere utilitarian backsplash into an undeniable focal point. And it's all done with basic square tiles; the pattern and color scheme make all the difference.

more about...

TILE

tile comes in a wide variety of shapes, sizes, textures, and colors, making it a good fit for any kitchen. More economical than slab or engineered stone, solid surfacing, or stainless steel, it can be the perfect DIY material too, although complex patterns might require an assist. Depending on the type of tile you choose, it may or may not need to be sealed. Glazed ceramic and glass titles, for instance, are nonporous but stone tile requires a sealer.

Likewise, cement-based grout—the most commonly used type—needs to be sealed to resist staining and mildew, preferably with a penetrating sealer. Epoxy and urethane grout don't require sealing and resist staining, although both take expertise to use, so consider hiring a professional. Your choice of grout color will have a visual impact too. White and dark grouts can make a tiled backsplash look busier; if you want a more subdued look, consider a gray-toned grout, even with white tile.

ABOVE When planning the perfect kitchen, sometimes all you need to do is go back to the basics. Marble countertops and subway tile are a hard combination to beat, as demonstrated in this white-on-white kitchen.

ABOVE Solid white field tiles make up the majority of this kitchen's backsplash but above the range, their decorative counterparts lend subtle pattern and texture.

LEFT Decorative tile creates a handsome backsplash throughout this kitchen, especially in back of the cooktop, where a bordered field behind the range is artlike in its appearance.

Mix 'n' match materials are at their best in this traditional kitchen, nowhere better than in the room's backsplash. Glass mosaic tiles in deep jewel tones wrap the majority of the room, while a field of ceramic tiles defines the cooking area.

The pattern of this variegated blue tile is more than a casual coincidence; it leads the eye to the pot filler over the stove.

more about...
INSTALLING GLASS TILE

glass tile has been a hot backsplash option for more than a decade and with all of the new colors and sizes available there are no signs of its popularity waning. Glass tiles are more reflective than their ceramic counterparts, though, and may reveal imperfections in the back board. Use white thinset compound with any ridges smoothed out before the tiles are set. Another installation tip: Glass tiles shouldn't be pushed together as tightly as ceramic tiles because glass reacts to temperature changes more dramatically.

Decorative tiles adorn the backsplash of this kitchen, its pattern making a dramatic impact in the midst of solid-color surfaces. The countertop tiles are heat-resistant, creating a perfectly suitable buffet space.

Glass tiles in varying sizes and colors create a backsplash that's just as handsome as it is tough. The cool color scheme is a good complement, as well, for the soft gray quartzite counter.

This concrete countertop was custom-designed with a stainless-steel drainboard set into it, allowing dishes to drip-dry and the water to run right into the sink.

more about...
CONCRETE

(i) f you're considering concrete countertops, your options reach far beyond gray. Concrete can take on almost any color, texture, or shape. Plus any number of objects can be cast into it, from glass bits to shells. The price you'll pay can vary greatly, depending on what aggregates or additives are in the concrete and how much complexity is involved. For either cast-in-place or precast concrete countertops, it's critical to find a reputable craftsperson.

Concrete's attributes include heat-resistance and durability, but it's just as heavy as stone, so account for the extra weight when choosing cabinets. And because concrete stains, it must be periodically sealed with a topical or penetrating sealer. Penetrating sealer results in a much more natural look and is best accompanied by periodic waxing to bring out the beauty of the material.

Thick concrete slabs top the counters in this kitchen, providing durable and heat-resistant surfaces. To keep it from staining, concrete must be sealed, but if done on a periodic basis, the material is easy to keep clean.

PAPER, GLASS, AND METAL COMPOSITES

the materials that go into today's composite countertops are wide ranging: Recycled metals, recycled paper and cardboard, glass, and even plant pulps—such as wheat paste and sorghum—are among those that you'll find. Some of the most popular composites are the following:

Paper-based composite countertops are made with recycled paper, newspaper, or cardboard, or with virgin paper, which results in a more uniform countertop. Paper-based countertops require finishing, but they won't off-gas and are heat-resistant, food safe, and strong. Scratches can be repaired by sanding, then reapplying the finish. There's good news for the do-it-yourselfer too; paper-based composites can be installed by a skilled homeowner.

Recycled glass countertops are indeed fabricated from recycled glass (sometimes including some virgin broken glass), which is mixed with cement binder or epoxy resin. Countertops made with cement binder are durable but do require sealing. Resin-bound countertops don't require sealing, just periodic waxing for shine. But because they're not quite as durable, it's a good idea not to cut on the resin-bound countertops.

Scrap metal countertops are typically made with aluminum shavings bound with resin, installed on a plywood substrate. Scrap metal composite counters don't require a sealer, but on the downside, they should not be cut on and are not heatproof.

Quartz, a form of engineered stone, is nonporous and resistant to heat, scratches, and stains. Here, quartz countertops team up with a backsplash of stacked stone tile, an equally hard worker in the kitchen.

The beauty of this unoiled Barroca™ soapstone countertop goes far beyond its appearance. The material—a combination of talc, quartz, and other minerals—is durable and heat-resistant, even to dishes right out of the oven.

more about...
SOLID SURFACING

Solid surfacing, made from polyester or acrylic resin mixed with a mineral filler and pigments, can be shaped to fit nearly any layout with the edge profile of your choice. In fact, solid-surface countertops can be fabricated with integral sinks and backsplashes. The material is completely nonporous, easy to clean, and moderately resistant to heat. Plus small scratches can be sanded out. (Larger abrasions require professional repair.)

Solid surfacing is available in a wide variety of colors and finishes as well as a wide range of prices. You can find patterns that look like stone, but you might also opt for one of the many bright, solid colors.

A blue engineered stone countertop lends a contemporary touch to this otherwise traditional kitchen. Behind the range, a handcrafted tile backsplash echoes the cool hue, providing a durable backdrop at the same time.

PLASTIC LAMINATE

plastic laminate remains a popular countertop material largely because it can be the most economical choice. Not only is it relatively stain proof, easy to clean, and waterproof—unless a seam is compromised—but it's DIY-friendly too. On the downside, it's relatively soft and scratches will show, so it's a good idea to use cutting boards. In addition, plastic laminate can't withstand super-hot pots and pans. If you are concerned about chemical sensitivity, look for low-VOC glues and substrates.

While plastic laminate may not be as glamorous as other countertop options, it's worth a closer look at today's range of patterns, colors, and finishes and variety of edge profiles. Edges can be beveled or bullnose or edged with materials like wood or metal. Choosing plastic laminate for perimeter counters could make room in your budget for a showpiece island countertop. An upgrade option is heavy-duty plastic laminate, which is fabricated with a thicker, tougher top layer. And be sure to consider an integral plastic-laminate sink.

An engineered stone countertop in this kitchen is right in step with the room's cool gray scheme. So is the metallic tile backsplash, for that matter, which adds a touch of sparkle in the process.

Countertops crafted of 2 in.-thick Calacatta slab marble establish an air of elegance in this kitchen, one that's taken a step further with the chevron mosaic backsplash that combines the Calacatta with the slightly darker Thassos marble.

more about...
ENGINEERED STONE OR QUARTZ COMPOSITE

engineered stone is technically a composite but it's primarily stone, made up of 90% stone chips and ground-stone powder. Because engineered stone is quartz based, it's often referred to as quartz or composite quartz, and countertops made of this material—due to the addition of resin in the mixture—are superior to slab stone in density. Plus they're extremely tough, hard to chip, heat-resistant, and need no sealing. Engineered stone comes in colors and patterns that are stonelike, but it's also fabricated in bright colors that you won't find in any other countertop material.

TOP LEFT Marble, like this countertop, is more often than not white but can come in other colors. In fact, as a metamorphosed limestone, marble gets its patterning from trace minerals, such as quartz and graphite.

LEFT Black CaesarStone countertops—one of the many types of quartz—provide a dramatic contrast to the white cabinetry in this kitchen. The material is stain- and scratch-resistant, and because it's nonporous, it doesn't need to be sealed.

ABOVE Italian soapstone does double-duty in this kitchen, serving as both the countertop and backsplash. Because the material gets darker over time, scratches can be more apparent early on but less so as time goes by.

RIGHT This slab of Jurassic Green granite has a stunning pattern. But it's important to always select slab stone in person because no two slabs will look alike.

SLAB STONE

When choosing a stone countertop or backsplash, it's imperative to visit stoneyards to see what you're getting; because no two stones are alike, you'll need to choose the exact slabs for your kitchen. And there are considerations beyond appearance. Review drawings by your designer and stone installer to understand where seams will go and ask how the slabs will be seamed. Vein-matched seams are made from two sequential slabs polished on the same face, while bookmatched seams are made from two sequential slabs polished on opposite faces so that they mirror each other when seamed.

If the price of slab stone doesn't fit into your budget, consider stone tiles instead. And prefab granite is another option. Cut and finished overseas, it's available only in standard sizes but in a variety of finishes and several edge profiles. Although it's thin and must be installed on ¾-in. plywood for strength, it's typically doubled at the edge to make it look like a thicker slab.

GRANITE

While granite has long been the countertop of choice in pricier kitchens, it's now made its way to those that are midrange too. Quarried in many countries—and in many colors, patterns, and prices—granite can be environmentally friendly, or not. Some granites may be available locally while others might be quarried in, say, South America and travel the ocean to another continent before making their way to your nearby stoneyard. Granite is extremely hard and durable; it's very tough to scratch. Plus it's cool to the touch and can withstand heat well. On the downside, it can be hard on dishes and can stain unless sealed regularly.

MARBLE AND LIMESTONE

Marble and limestone have seductive good looks, making them worth the extra effort needed to use them as countertops. Marble's cool temperature is ideal for rolling pastry dough. Just be aware that while marble isn't likely to stain if properly and regularly sealed, acidic foods will etch it, even if spills are wiped up immediately. A honed surface won't show scratches as much as a polished surface. But if you do prefer a polished surface, just consider small scratches part of the patina that marble develops in a well-used kitchen. Limestone is softer and even more susceptible to etching than marble, but it can make a beautiful countertop in a lesser-used area—or a beautiful backsplash anywhere.

SLATE AND SOAPSTONE

Slate and soapstone come in smaller slabs than granite, and in more limited colors. Still, both can make beautiful, durable countertops that require less care than many types of granite. Slate varies in density, and not all slates are suitable for countertops. But both countertop-worthy slate and soapstone are denser and less porous than granite, and most do not require sealing. The color of slate depends on where it's quarried, with hues ranging from black to green to red. Soapstone is light in tone when quarried and polished, but oxidizes over time and turns dark, and veining becomes more prominent. You can speed up the darkening process by rubbing soapstone with mineral oil, boiled linseed oil, or a food-safe beeswax, with more applications early on and fewer as time goes by. A bonus of soapstone darkening is that scratches are less apparent.

sinks

● ● ● YOU MIGHT BE SURPRISED BY THE TOTAL if you actually added up how many hours you spend standing at a sink, so it's important to choose wisely and position strategically. For starters, locate the main sink where you have a good view; in front of a window is a traditional option, but overlooking the kitchen or family room can work well too. Provide 2 ft. on each side of the main sink, one side for dirty dishes and the other for clean. And consider adding a prep or bar sink, if there's room in both the kitchen and the budget. A prep sink should be close to the cooktop and the main work surface, or it can be the centerpiece of a secondary prep area. If your two sinks are somewhat far apart, locate the trash between them or consider two trash centers. Once you've decided how many sinks you want, determine the configuration and what type will work best with your countertop. Finally, always shop for faucets at the same time that you shop for sinks.

A farmhouse sink like this ensures that even the largest pots and pans will fit. Its generous width also provides plenty of room for assorted faucets, sprayers, and dispensers.

ABOVE A custom-fabricated soapstone sink and matching countertop create a seamless look in this kitchen, while a refurbished antique pendant casts a glow on the impressive basin. Meanwhile, a faucet in a nickel finish has an appropriately vintage feeling.

LEFT A prep sink, like this stainless-steel version, is a good idea in a large kitchen or in one where two cooks regularly work together. This undermount style tucks beneath the quartzite countertop of the island.

LEFT The simplicity of this double-basin, stainless-steel sink is matched by the single-lever gooseneck faucet. Likewise, the surround of black-honed slate—used for the countertops, backsplash, and low windowsills—is the epitome of understated elegance.

FACING PAGE The farmhouse-style sink in this kitchen is set below counter height, making it easier to reach into. The poured-in-place concrete countertop surrounding it features a handy dish drain on one side.

more about...
SINK MATERIALS

Stainless steel has a lot going for it. This unpretentious material is nonporous, easy to clean, durable, immune to heat, and comes in a wide range of sizes, configurations, and prices. A 6-in.-deep, rectangular, single-bowl, 18-gauge model is a popular choice, and it's big enough for larger pots and pans. But a 16-gauge sink is sturdier; the lower the gauge number, the thicker the steel. Look for a number 4 brushed surface too, as polished stainless steel is harder to keep clean. With the wide variety of available sink configurations, it's likely you'll find one to fit your needs. If not, you can hire a local shop to fabricate a custom design.

Copper, nickel, and bronze sinks can be stunning, but the cost is high, sometimes prohibitively. Plus their upkeep is far more demanding than for stainless steel. An alternative to regularly polishing copper is to let it oxidize, creating an ever-changing patina.

Solid-surface sinks are not cheap, but they have their definite advantages. They're nonporous and stain-resistant; plus small scratches won't show up because the material is homogenous. Modest scratches can be sanded out, and a licensed fabricator can even repair more serious damage.

Acrylic sinks are inexpensive, nonporous, and available in a number of configurations. Still, they are susceptible to abrasive cleaners and petroleum-based products. In addition, they can't

stand the heat of pots straight from the cooktop. Look for higher-end acrylic sinks that claim to resist staining and scratching.

Enameled sinks are easy to clean. And difficult to scratch. They can, however, chip and potentially expose the metal to rust. Keep in mind too that enameled cast-iron is unforgiving on dropped glasses, although you can avoid that by placing a metal rack in the bottom of the sink. Enameled steel sinks are much lighter than cast iron and typically less expensive.

Stone can be carved into a sink, but a stone sink is more likely to be fabricated from flat slabs, creating an apron-front configuration. Soapstone, for instance, is a traditional sink material that's easy to work with and it's relatively gentle on dropped dishes. Keep in mind, however, that any stone sink requires extra support.

Engineered stone sinks are made of a mix of powdered stone (usually quartz or granite) and a small amount of resin. These sinks are tough, strong, don't need sealing, and won't stain.

Ceramic sinks can be cast with intricate details. But they are heavy, hard on dropped dishes, and susceptible to cracks if hot water is poured into a cold sink or a hot pan is set on it. A metal grid that fits into the bottom of the sink can prevent dings, broken dishware, and even thwart heat-related cracking.

•sink configurations

The most versatile of sinks is 33 in. wide and 10 in. deep with a single bowl, one that's big enough for large cookie sheets and stockpots. (If you go wider than a 33 in. sink, know that it will require a wider-than-standard sink base cabinet.) Be aware, however, that sinks with wide-radiused inside corners may look more spacious than they really are; their inside measurements may not be able to accommodate larger items. To be on the safe side, take a couple of your favorite large pots and pans to the showroom when shopping or at least know the dimensions of your pieces.

On the other hand, if every pot and pan goes straight into the dishwasher, a two-bowl sink may work just fine. Whatever type you choose, consider where the drain is located. Most sinks have centered drains but a drain off to the side will make it easier to soak a pan. For sink installation options, see the facing page.

Side-by-side sinks, with the countertop material separating the two, create the illusion of a double basin. The primary faucet, positioned between the two, easily accommodates both.

SINK INSTALLATION TYPES

DROP-IN OR SELF-RIMMING SINK

Countertop materials that have a vulnerable edge, such as plastic laminate and wood, require a self-rimming sink (although integrated plastic-laminate sinks are available in some limited styles). Steel sinks can be clipped into place and trimmed with a separate piece or are self-rimming, the latter a neater but more expensive option. And porcelain-enamel cast-iron sinks remain in place by their sheer weight. Keep in mind that the lip around a self-rimming sink can be hard to keep clean. All drop-in and self-mounting sinks should be sealed under the lip with silicone caulk.

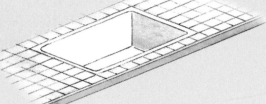

FLUSH-MOUNT SINK

Flush-mount sinks are designed to drop in onto the substrate and flush with a tile countertop. Tile is installed flush with the sink, which may require shimming to align properly with the tile. Caulk between the tile and the edge of the sink makes the joint waterproof.

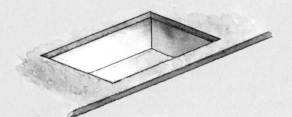

UNDERMOUNT SINK

Undermount sinks make it easy to clean off the countertop but require a little extra attention to keep the inside top edge of the sink clean. The potentially tricky part of installation lies in cutting the hole for it properly, either off-site or in place. Countertop materials that require sealing must be sealed at the cut edge. And because the sink is set lower than a drop-in sink, its greater depth will require you to bend over more.

INTEGRAL SINK

Integral sinks are built right into countertops, or at least have that appearance; they have either no joints or tightly glued joints, so they don't leak or have joints to clean around. Stainless steel or other metals—either shopmade or manufactured—come in many configurations of integral sink, backsplash, and countertop. Solid-surface, composite stone, and some plastic laminate countertops can be shop fabricated with integral sinks.

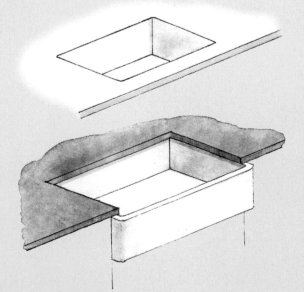

FARMHOUSE OR APRON-FRONT SINK

The farmhouse, or apron-front, sink protrudes from the countertop and cabinetry, making it easier to get close to whatever produce or dishes you're washing. Farmhouse sinks tend to be more costly, however, both for the fixture and for the required special cabinet below.

faucets

● ● ● CHOOSE FAUCETS AT THE SAME TIME YOU select sinks and countertops, in part to coordinate styles and colors but, more important, to make sure dimensions are compatible. A sink that takes up lots of countertop space from front to back may not leave room for every make of faucet, or space to clean around it, for that matter. One way to give a faucet more breathing room is to bump out the sink cabinet, creating a deeper countertop. Faucets can be deck mounted behind the sink, either on the countertop or on a ledge built into the sink itself. Or they can be wall mounted, a configuration that makes it much easier to clean between sink and backsplash.

Most of today's kitchen faucets have a single lever or handle, requiring that just one hole be cut into the countertop or sink ledge. A separate sprayer, soap dispenser, or water filter will require additional holes, even as many as five if you have a faucet, sprayer, soap dispenser, cold-water filter, and instant hot-water dispenser.

ABOVE A sprayer pulls out from this lever-controlled faucet, making it easy to direct water anywhere in the deep sink below.

RIGHT The design of this contemporary kitchen is based on straight lines and angles, right down to the faucet at the prep sink. The single-lever style is just as understated as the rest of the room.

The gooseneck faucet teamed with this double-basin sink features a flared spray head and a coil-spring neck, making it easier to clean large dishes and cookware. The water dispenser to the right of the faucet echoes the graceful curve of the main faucet.

FAUCET MATERIALS

When shopping for faucets, the best ones you'll find have stainless steel or brass bodies. Stainless-steel faucets require no coating and are either highly polished or brushed but are considerably more expensive than brass-bodied faucets. Brass faucets are always coated, most commonly with chrome (which is easy to keep looking clean) or with nickel (which is warmer in tone and more historically authentic but prone to spotting). As a rule, a brushed finish makes for easier cleanup than one that's shiny, but there's something about a gleaming, polished-chrome faucet that still makes it a popular choice.

RIGHT Traditional style is at its best in this brushed-brass bridge faucet—complete with cross handles and matching sprayer.

ABOVE At a prep sink, where fruits and vegetables are constantly being washed, it's important to have a sprayer close at hand. This pull-down version can reach down into the sink, keeping water splash to a minimum.

FACING PAGE A pot-filler located over the cooktop eliminates the need to carry a full pot of water the entire way across the kitchen. This one draws the eye to the decorative tile backsplash as well.

FAUCET AND SPRAYER CHOICES

LEVER, SINGLE HANDLE

A single-lever faucet has a lower arc than a gooseneck faucet, with the lever positioned behind and above the spout. These are easier to reach than side-mounted handles, which are the norm for gooseneck, high-arch spouts. But gooseneck spouts are popular for their looks as well as the ability to set a tall pot in the sink for washing. Some homeowners prefer to move the side-mounted handle to the front, making it easier to operate.

THE HANDS-FREE FAUCET

Especially popular with serious cooks, a hands-free faucet is operated by a motion sensor or a foot pedal or lever. Either device can be turned off as needed, and a foot pedal can be locked on for a continuous stream, then unlocked to control the water with your foot again. Another bonus is this: A hands-free faucet means fewer fingerprints and water spots on the spout and handle.

SPRAYERS

A faucet and sprayer can be installed as separate elements but today's homeowners prefer pull-down sprayers by a wide margin. The head of the faucet pulls down to become a sprayer attached to a flexible hose, extending the reach of the faucet by a significant amount. Furthermore, most faucet sprayers change from stream to spray with the touch of a button.

appliances

• • •

GIVEN TODAY'S PLETHORA OF APPLIANCES, CHOOSING THE RIGHT ones for your kitchen may not be as easy as it seems. Is a range best for your daily routine or would a cooktop and wall oven be a better fit? Likewise, would you prefer a combined refrigerator/freezer or are separate units more appealing? Even selecting a dishwasher isn't as simple as it once was; dishwasher drawers now offer an alternative to more conventional units. Plus with today's hurry-up lifestyles, microwaves are all but status quo but maybe you'd prefer to use that space for a coffee center. All of these appliances will claim a hefty chunk of your kitchen budget. Although online shopping makes it easier than ever to compare before you buy, don't forget that floor and closeout models are often good bargains. Keep in mind too that most appliances are more energy-efficient today, which can mean increased savings over time.

When purchasing any appliance, it's important to coordinate the specifications with existing cabinets; for new construction, coordinate before the cabinets are built or bought. By the same token, plumbing and electrical layouts must coordinate too. (Keep in mind that steam ovens, coffee centers, and refrigerators with icemakers or water dispensers require water that tastes good—not just potable water—so consider a centralized water filter to handle them all.) Finally, be sure that cabinet and appliance doors can fully open without interference from walls or other doors.

What could have been awkward angles in this kitchen instead perfectly showcase a stainless-steel range and hood. The dual-fuel range offers the best of two worlds—a gas cooktop and electric ovens.

cooking appliances

●●● DECIDING WHAT TYPE OF COOKING appliance is best for your kitchen should be based on more than your personal preference. You, for instance, might prefer a range, whether it's a basic, space-saving model or a focal-point piece with multiple burners and fuel sources. But a two-cook kitchen may be better served by separate units, perhaps a cooktop, one or more wall ovens, even a specialized oven or two. Separate cooking appliances require additional installation but they also offer more flexibility. Wall ovens can fit into a bank of wall cabinets or tuck under a countertop. Smaller ovens—including microwave, steam, speed, and warming ovens—can fit into cabinetry above a wall oven but often function more comfortably when placed under the countertop.

ABOVE A pair of stacked wall ovens, with a built-in microwave to the right, makes this cooking area a model of efficiency. A landing area is essential for any oven; here, a nearby island fills the bill.

LEFT This configuration, with a microwave directly over the range, keeps cooking appliances conveniently in one central location. Given the variegated gray tones of the tile backsplash, the stainless-steel appliances are a good fit for the room's color scheme too.

This gas cooktop has its own stainless-steel backsplash as well as a matching hood. Drawers directly beneath it provide a convenient place to store all kinds of cooking utensils.

FACING PAGE A sleek cooktop, as well as ovens tucked under the counter, are in keeping with the streamlined style of this contemporary kitchen, as is the glass and stainless-steel hood.

RIGHT This stainless-steel range and hood are visually tied together by a checkerboard backsplash of the same material. Plus the hood does more than provide an updraft; built-in lighting and pot racks are bonuses.

BELOW Smooth-to-the-touch cooktops like this one come in electric and induction models; the latter is more energy-efficient than its electric counterpart. An induction cooktop also allows instant heat control, much like gas, which is preferred by many cooks.

•ranges

For years, cooks had to make a choice between gas and electric ranges; gas delivered a speedy response but electric had the advantage of steady temperatures. But those days are long gone. Today's ranges offer dual-fuel options, even on the cooktop itself. And range configurations have changed to suit the times too, with some moderately priced models featuring a warming drawer or two stacked ovens.

It's important to note that some ranges are taller and deeper than the typical base cabinet and countertop. Likewise, a free-standing range may not fit perfectly into a spot where a slide-in once was. Compare your own situation to exact product specs and inquire about filler pieces and retrofit options. It's easier to accommodate bigger ranges in new cabinetry, as base cabinets can be installed an inch or two away from the wall (which will require deeper countertops) or on higher toe space bases.

True commercial ranges belong in commercial kitchens, not homes; they can be extremely hot to the touch, even to the point of scorching adjacent cabinets. But professional-style ranges like this are insulated and have pilotless ignitions, plus consumer-friendly features such as oven windows, oven lights, and broilers.

ⓖⓐⓛⓛⓔⓡⓨ

a range of colors

There was a time when you had but three range colors from which to choose: Black, white, and stainless-steel gray. But professional-style ranges are now available in a rainbow of colors.

Proof that the same range can take on two entirely different looks: A robin's egg–blue model, surrounded by white cabinetry, has cottage appeal, whereas the cherry-red version, flanked by sage-green cabinets, takes on a more straightforward traditional style.

A focal point amid an otherwise neutral setting, this bright red gas range has a definitively modern look. A convenient, built-in storage drawer adds to its appeal.

This deep blue range—featuring double ovens—takes color to another level; the extra-wide appliance plus a matching hood multiplies the dramatic impact.

•ovens

The standard oven is a radiant, or thermal oven, which cooks by a combination of radiant energy from a heat source—an electric element at the bottom and top (for broiling) or a gas-fired flame under the oven floor. Convection ovens incorporate a fan in an electric radiant oven, and a true convection oven has a third heating element that heats the air before it circulates, making it more efficient.

If you tend to cook different foods at different temperatures, two ovens may serve you better than one. Wall ovens are available at all price points, and some 30-in. and 36-in. ranges offer two ovens, typically stacked. Larger pro-style ranges and heavy-duty European models, meanwhile, have several small ovens both stacked and side by side. Keep in mind, however, that a smaller oven is more energy efficient and retains moisture better.

Featuring multiple functions, this built-in oven truly does it all, not only providing microwave options but also speed, warming, and convection alternatives.

more about...
WARMING DRAWERS AND SPECIALTY OVENS

a warming oven, also referred to as a warming drawer, can keep foods at an optimal temperature while the rest of dinner is being prepared. But they can serve more than their prime purpose. Warming drawers are also convenient for warming plates, proofing bread dough, defrosting food, and even drying breadcrumbs. A range with a built-in warming drawer can be an economical option, but consider convenience too. A separate warming drawer can be positioned at a more comfortable level, such as just under the countertop.

Speed and steam ovens are two other increasingly popular options. Speed ovens can incorporate microwave energy, steam, convection, and high-intensity radiant heat, such as halogen bulbs. Steam ovens incorporate

steam from a reservoir or plumbed water line (the latter is more expensive) while the hybrid steam-convection oven provides the best of both technologies. You might first steam a chicken to make it tender and juicy, and then give it a crispy skin via convection. Plus either function can be used alone.

Don't neglect single task options, either. A built-in coffee center may have a narrow focus but might be just the thing to ease a busy morning schedule. Many systems require no water supply so they can be located anywhere; a plumbed water supply is more convenient but will be more costly. Finally, if you have a teenager in the house, a countertop pizza oven is not a bad idea, either.

MICROWAVE OVENS

@ microwave oven is considered essential in most kitchens, given today's fast-paced lifestyles. Some homeowners, in fact, go so far as to think of it as the primary oven, especially as new technologies—such as convection and steam heat—are being incorporated. An over-the-range microwave makes sense in a small kitchen, creating one compact cooking area. But in a larger kitchen, consider a location that's out of the path of the primary cook, especially if other family members are inclined to use it while meals are being prepped. Built-in microwaves tend to be deeper than wall cabinets but will fit neatly into base cabinets or a deep wall of cabinets that includes an oven or two. Microwave drawers also fit into base cabinets, ideally at the end of a run of cabinets or in an island, away from the main cooking zone and with a landing area immediately above.

You can also give a freestanding model a built-in look by creating a custom niche in a base cabinet. Just be sure to provide an outlet at the back plus room for the cord.

TOP LEFT A microwave atop a wall oven stacks up to convenience in this kitchen. In a situation like this, in which the oven doors open toward a counter, be sure to allow room for a person to pass through when the doors are fully extended.

LEFT The placement of this microwave oven is ideal. Set into a cabinet at the edge of the kitchen, it doesn't interfere with the main cooking area yet is convenient to cooks and noncooks alike.

•cooktops

Cooktops are fueled in one of two ways—by gas (natural or propane) or electricity. The cost of power and availability of gas may factor into which cooktop you choose. When making a selection, know that there are several electric options; they can be inexpensive electric coil, standard electric smooth top, or electro-magnetic-powered induction.

There is no standard configuration for cooktops; it will vary widely depending on the overall width and fuel source. Still, there are some basic guidelines. Look for a cooktop that has at least two high-powered burners and one that can simmer steadily. Some models offer two large burners in front, but most offer one large burner and one smaller burner in front and the reverse configuration in back. Conventional electric cooktops may offer bridge elements, which tie together two burners to make a single one large enough to accommodate a roasting pan—perfect if you're making gravy. Likewise, a gas cooktop might feature a continuous grate that also makes it easy to handle that wide roasting pan.

Cooktops can be installed into a countertop like a drop-in sink—with the countertop surrounding it on all sides—or like an apron-front sink, with the countertop interrupted by the unit. Take care that any backsplash behind a cooktop is resistant to heat, as well as moisture and stains. Allow for a landing space that's at least 9 in. on one side and 15 in. on the other, with 9 in. behind the cooktop if it's on an island or peninsula. If there's bar seating behind the cooktop, provide at least 24 in. of space.

This low-profile cooktop practically disappears from sight, as does its accompanying hood. The stainless-steel element blends quietly into the backdrop, creating a soothing ambience.

The hood over this cooktop serves more than one practical purpose. Not only does it provide ventilation but a shelf at the front and pot rack at the back keep all kinds of essentials close at hand.

An apron-front cooktop features controls on the front; because they're easy to access, the cooktop is a good universal design option. The hardwood floor also adheres to the principles of universal design, as it's an easy surface on which to roll a wheelchair.

more about...
GAS COOKTOPS

u ntil the induction cooktop came along, the gas cooktop was considered far superior to its electric counterpart for its instant, infinite control. Still, gas has its advantages over induction. It typically stays on during power outages and can be less expensive than induction—sometimes significantly. A gas cooktop doesn't require iron-based cookware; instead, you'll find specialized accessories, such as a grill, griddle, and deep fryer. But when it comes right down to it, you don't have to decide between gas and induction. Some gas cooktops incorporate an induction element or two.

All of the cooking appliances keep a low profile in this kitchen. In the island, a gas cooktop teams up with an oven directly beneath it; a second oven—also set under the counter—is nearby, teamed with a built-in microwave.

more about...
ELECTRIC COOKTOPS

Standard electric coil cooktops, as well as smooth-top models, heat up quickly. The downside, however, is that they are slow to respond to temperature changes. Smooth tops have the advantage of being easier to clean than coils, especially if spills are attended to quickly. Dark surfaces hide dirt better than white ones, but all ceramic glass smooth tops are prone to scratches from heavy pots and pans.

more about...
INDUCTION COOKTOPS

induction cooktops are powered by electromagnetic energy, which causes iron-based cookware (such as cast iron and stainless steel) to heat up. The burners are topped by a ceramic glass surface and are more energy efficient—almost twice as much—than either gas or electric cooktops. Plus they provide consistent heat, are quick to respond, and offer easy cleanup; spilled food won't burn and stick to the cooktop, which is cool to the touch. (But while the burner itself is cool there can be residual heat from the hot pot itself.) This makes the induction cooktop a good choice if you want to adhere to universal design standards.

Induction cooktops do require flat-bottomed iron-based cookware. If you aren't sure that you want to commit completely to induction cooking, look for cooktops that combine gas or standard burners with one or two induction burners.

The cooktop in this kitchen is just as smooth to the touch—and easy to clean— as the glossy white island that it's set in.

•cooktop ventilation

Good ventilation is essential to any cooktop. A ducted vent draws cooking smells, smoke, moisture, and airborne grease away from the cooktop; grease is then captured while moisture and smoke are blown outside. A ductless hood vent filters grease and moisture, and then re-circulates the air back into the kitchen.

A built-in downdraft cooktop vent, which has a fan mounted under the cooktop, can pop up or be surface mounted. Pop-ups are better at venting than surface-mounted models, simply because they are physically closer to the tops of pots and pans. Both types of downdraft vents are less visible—and typically less expensive—than an updraft vent hood, but they may not be strong enough for high-intensity cooking. An over-the-range microwave oven with a ventilation hood isn't ideal but if a microwave/vent is your choice, select a ducted model and vent it to the outdoors. Cooktops in islands are popular but be aware that venting an island or peninsula cooktop will require a stronger fan than a cooktop against a wall, as the wall helps direct heat, moisture, and grease to the hood.

A fan's strength—along with the hood's size, placement, and configuration—influence the effectiveness of a ventilation system. A hood should ideally be about 3 in. wider than the cooktop to scoop air most effectively, even wider on an island cooktop. And the higher the hood above the cooktop, the wider it should be. Make sure, as well, that ducts are smooth and have as few bends as possible.

ABOVE Set in the island of this contemporary kitchen, the cooktop is teamed with a suspended hood that's powerful enough to properly ventilate the area.

FACING PAGE A single hood serves this split cooktop, creating—along with the built-in niche below—a sense of continuity. A bank of wall ovens is just steps away, keeping the cooking zone in one compact area.

LEFT Dispelling the notion that a hood is purely practical, this one showcases a collection of vintage bottles—the perfect touch in this country-style kitchen.

gallery

hood styles

Many hoods are impressive design features in their own right, creating dramatic focal points in today's kitchens.

Coupled with a decorative tile backsplash, this black-and-white hood—with graceful curves—makes a dramatic design statement.

Hoods can be crafted to any size and shape. The face of this custom, white-painted model echoes the design of the cabinets below.

Reflecting the materials of the range below, this barrel-shaped metal hood is accented with riveted metal straps.

The copper hood over this cooktop can be polished from time to time to retain its gleaming finish, or if left untreated, it will develop a verde green patina.

In keeping with the rustic style of this kitchen, a reclaimed beam set into the white tile surround conceals ventilation. The decorative tile of the backsplash balances the straightforward design element.

BELOW Stainless steel is undoubtedly the most popular finish for today's refrigerator/freezers. Here, it seems a particularly good fit for the cool blue-gray color scheme, but the real beauty of stainless is that it goes with anything.

RIGHT This refrigerator/freezer is faced with panels that perfectly match the cabinetry, allowing it to blend quietly into the background. Even the hardware matches that of the adjacent base cabinets.

refrigerators and freezers

●●● REFRIGERATORS AND FREEZERS HAVE seen numerous changes over time, nowhere more so than in configuration and efficiency. Today, their interiors are finely tuned, fitted with drawers, moveable shelves, variable temperatures, and electric controls. Likewise, exteriors have evolved. Stainless steel, one of the most popular options, adds to the price of a refrigerator, and it's harder to keep clean than more-conventional black and white finishes. Still, it adds a professional gleam to a kitchen. A brushed finish doesn't show fingerprints like polished stainless steel, which may be more appealing. Many refrigerators and freezers can be faced with panels to match your cabinetry too, giving them more of a low-profile look.

Today, you'll also find options beyond conventional, twin bed–size appliances. Refrigerator and freezer drawers are increasingly popular, as are undercounter refrigerators and trash compactor–size ice makers.

more about...
FITTING IN THE FRIDGE

how your refrigerator fits into the kitchen will be a matter of your budget and what appeals to you aesthetically. The standard refrigerator is 27 in. deep, 3 in. deeper than the standard 24-in.-deep cabinet. You might opt for a freestanding cabinet-depth (about 24 in.) refrigerator, although it will cost a bit more. More expensive still is a built-in refrigerator, with or without panels that match your cabinetry. Finally, the highest-price option is an integrated refrigerator; completely covered by cabinetry, it has no visible seams or edges.

If it's important to you that the cabinets and refrigerator align, there are a couple of options. Cabinet-depth refrigerators make it easier to locate and retrieve food but, on the other hand, they may not accommodate a baking sheet. (That's why it's important to measure your platters and take those measurements with you to the appliance showroom.) Another approach is to set standard cabinets a few inches away from the wall to align with a standard-depth refrigerator. In either case, be sure to provide landing space on the opening side—at least 15 in.—or a countertop across from it.

Tucked out of the way in one corner of this kitchen, a pair of refrigerator drawers is topped by a wine refrigerator. They're easily accessible for someone chatting with the cook without getting in his or her way.

ENERGY-WISE IDEAS
FOR REFRIGERATORS

refrigerators continue to get more efficient, thanks to stronger and stronger energy standards. When shopping for a refrigerator, check those you're considering against the energy statistics found on the Energy Guide, a yellow tag that's available in showrooms and in product literature online. Note that Energy Star® ratings compare refrigerators in the same category, and that some configurations are considerably more energy efficient than others.

Top-freezer refrigerators are the most energy efficient, while side-by-side models are the least. For bottom freezers, look for a two-drawer model so frozen items don't get deeply buried. And keep in mind that in-door ice and water dispensers will add 15% or more to your energy bill. Of course, the biggest contributor to energy use is the refrigerator's size, so opt for something smaller if it will work for you.

Whatever configuration you choose, keep in mind that the easier it is to retrieve food, the less time the door stays open, so consider models with pull-out shelves, see-through drawers, and good lighting. Keep refrigerators away from heat-generating appliances, and make sure there's enough air space around all appliances to vent ambient heat.

ABOVE The undisputable highlight of this kitchen, a light blue refrigerator—with a refrigerator on top and a freezer on the bottom—has retro appeal in both its color and configuration.

RIGHT This integrated refrigerator is wrapped in the same rich wood grain as the rest of the room's cabinetry, making it as much a design element as it is a practical appliance.

more about...
WINE REFRIGERATORS

a built-in undercounter wine refrigerator is basically the size of a dishwasher, holding 28 to 60 bottles, depending on the size of the bottle. Most built-in models are stainless steel with glass-paneled doors, but some—like standard refrigerators—can be paneled to match the cabinetry. While a built-in wine refrigerator vents out the front, freestanding models typically vent out the rear, so they should not be completely built into cabinetry.

Located in a butler's pantry between the kitchen and dining room, this wine refrigerator is easily accessible while entertaining. The pull-out drawers inside allow bottles to be neatly organized.

This undercounter refrigerator keeps all manner of beverages cold. It's smartly located near wall cabinets filled with glassware as well as a stainless-steel sink.

dishwashers

● ● ● YOU'D THINK LOCATING A DISHWASHER would be a no-brainer: Put it next to the sink. But which side of the sink? Are you left-handed or right? If you're considering dishwasher drawers, think about placing one on each side of the sink; this arrangement adheres to universal design, as it doesn't require bending over as far to load and unload dishes. Another universal design suggestion is to install the dishwasher 6 in. to 10 in. above floor level. Ideally, dish storage should be within easy reach of the dishwasher, making it a one-step process to empty the dishwasher.

The standard dishwasher is 24 in. wide although 18-in. models are available for tight spaces; extra-wide dishwashers are available too. When deciding what size is best for you, take some of your most-used dishes to the showroom to test a variety of rack configurations. Some dishwashers have racks that can move down, making room for plates on the top, while others have tines that fold out of the way to make room for pots and pans. Some manufacturers even offer a steam option, which is a gentle way to wash fragile stemware.

ABOVE Because this kitchen is part of a great room where entertaining takes place, the fact that the dishwasher features sound insulation is a plus; it can be run whether company is on hand or not. Concealed controls give it a streamlined look.

RIGHT This kitchen features an efficient arrangement, with a dishwasher on the left side of the sink and a trash compactor on the right. Plus there's plenty of cupboard space above the dishwasher, making it easy to put away dishes in one simple move.

FACING PAGE RIGHT An efficient bar tucked into this niche incorporates not only the requisite sink and plenty of cabinet space for barware; there's also an undercounter wine refrigerator as well as a dishwasher.

ENERGY-WISE IDEAS FOR DISHWASHERS

federal standards have improved the efficiency of dishwashers greatly. Study the yellow Energy Guide label for comparative energy use, knowing that Energy Star models will be your best bet; they use about two-thirds less water than those that don't make the grade.

Whatever dishwasher you choose, you can save both water and energy by letting it do its job. A dishwasher uses less water—and less heat—than handwashing, so scrape food off plates and put them in the dishwasher,

unrinsed. Wash full loads too, and keep in mind that air-drying dishes uses less energy than heat drying.

You'll find that today's dishwashers are smarter too. Many have sensors that analyze the water at certain points in the cycle, then adjust the water and detergent accordingly. Some even boast a favorite-cycle feature, which lets you preprogram your machine to automatically select options that you use the most.

floors, walls, and ceilings

● ● ●

WHEN PLANNING A KITCHEN, IT'S EASY TO GET CAUGHT UP IN THE allure of handsome cabinetry and high-tech appliances. But floors, walls, and ceilings represent a great share of the square footage and thus deserve to be more than a mere afterthought. A kitchen floor, for instance, needs to be serviceable. It should resist stains and water, withstand the dings of dropped dinnerware, and stand up to heavy traffic. In addition, considering how much time is spent there, it needs to be easy on the feet and back. That's a lot to ask, but you'll also want your kitchen floor to look good, especially if it's part of a great room.

Similarly, your kitchen walls should be aesthetically pleasing and stand up to food and water stains. Plus surfaces behind the stove need to be heat-resistant. The good news is that there are a wide variety of kitchen-appropriate materials, from paint and wallpaper to tile and beadboard paneling. Select colors and textures that will complement your cabinetry and appliances, and—in a space often dominated by one-color elements—perhaps add a touch of pattern too.

There are multiple options for the ceiling, as well, beyond basic paint. Consider rustic beams for a country-style kitchen or apply wallpaper to add a splash of pattern. You might even add an architectural touch by shaping the space with a coffered or paneled ceiling.

Plain white field tiles team up with patterned coordinates to create the look of an area rug in this kitchen. Not only is it a good-looking design solution but it's easier to clean than a rug.

floors

●●● WHEN SELECTING A FLOOR SURFACE for your kitchen, consider three basic criteria: How does it look, how well does it work, and how does it make you feel—physically—at the end of the day? There's often an instant connection with aesthetics; most homeowners quickly know if they like a floor material or not. But is it hard-wearing and easy to keep clean? For durability and longevity, nonresilient materials such as ceramic and stone tile are long lasting. But on the downside, neither is comfortable to stand on for long stretches at a time. If comfort is your key criterion, choose a softer material such as resilient (cork, vinyl, linoleum, or rubber), laminate, or wood flooring. Wood is a particularly popular option not only because it's warm and comfortable but also because it can make a kitchen blend seamlessly into a living space.

The hardwood floor in this kitchen is not only a handsome contrast for the sage-green cabinetry but also seamlessly connects the kitchen with the breakfast nook (not shown), underscored by the same material.

FAR LEFT The weathered ash finish of this oak flooring takes the same light approach as the rest of the room. The random planks are a good fit for the traditional styling throughout.

LEFT The warmth of wood is the main attraction in this kitchen, all the way down to the floor. Because floors—and walls and ceilings, for that matter—cover so much square footage, they make a big impact.

ABOVE The flooring in this kitchen is right in step with the two-tone approach of the room. Almost everything above counter level is light and bright while; below, it's subdued and stylish.

more about...
WOOD FLOORING

because it's warm and resilient, and can be refinished again and again, wood flooring is a perennial favorite. The majority of **solid-wood** flooring is oak strip (¾ in. thick and 2½ in. wide); wider planks are available but are more expensive. Other options include hardwoods such as maple, cherry, and hickory. Softwoods like heart pine and fir are handsome too, but they are more susceptible to dents and dings. **Engineered wood** has the look of solid wood but consists of a thin layer of solid appearance-grade wood laminated to several layers of plywood, making it more dimensionally stable than its solid counterpart. It can, however, be a challenge to refinish engineered flooring because the top layer is so thin.

Both solid- and engineered-wood flooring can be prefinished or unfinished (although engineered wood flooring is almost always prefinished). Prefinished wood flooring is durable and ready to walk on as soon as it's installed, but the joints can be vulnerable to water damage. Finishing wood flooring in place takes time, emanates odors, and requires staying off it for a few days. Although this option isn't quite as hard wearing as a factory finish, it provides better overall protection because the joints are sealed along with the strips.

Any kind of wood requires frequent vacuuming and damp mopping, as well as quick attention to spills. You'll find too that glossy finishes and dark tones will show scratches and stains more than medium tones and satin finishes.

RESILIENT FLOORING

resilient flooring is a favorite in kitchens; it's comfortable to stand on, easy to install, and relatively inexpensive. Plus it can last for years if well maintained—sweeping and damp mopping to remove grit, and wiping up spills from seams quickly. Most resilient flooring comes in both tiles and sheets, while others are available as floating-floor planks or tiles that snap together without an adhesive.

Cork flooring is considered sustainable because the bark is peeled from a live tree without damaging the tree itself. It's quiet and resilient, and repels mold and mildew, making it particularly attractive for those who are chemically sensitive.

Rubber flooring is made from recycled rubber products and thus is relatively green. Available in a variety of colors and textures, rubber is durable, comfortable, and easy to clean. It is rather pricey, though, compared to other resilient floorings.

Vinyl flooring is the least expensive of all resilient flooring options, but it's not the shiny no-wax flooring that it once was. Today, it's typically made of a tough outer coating, a clear vinyl layer, a printed design or color layer (much like laminate flooring), and a bottom layer of felt or fiberglass. Vinyl is available in large sheets or tiles; sheets offer more water resistance because there are fewer seams.

Linoleum flooring, made up of linseed oil, wood flour, limestone, tree resins, and jute—all naturally available—is relatively easy to manufacture. With a solvent-free adhesive, it's one of the greenest flooring materials around; it's completely biodegradable or recyclable. Like other resilient floorings, linoleum is soft underfoot and easy to install. Unlike vinyl, however, it's homogenous throughout.

ABOVE A well-worn hardwood floor can be given a new lease on life with a simple coat of paint. A sealer is particularly important, so the paint—in this case a checkerboard pattern—doesn't wear away.

LEFT Laminate flooring has a lot going for it, especially in a kitchen. It is comparatively inexpensive, easy to install, comfortable to stand on, and easy to clean.

Red lacquer–stained cabinets team with a dark gray island and built-in refrigerator in this kitchen. The gray also makes its way to the floor in the form of concrete inlays. Blond ash wood adds eye-catching contrast.

more about...
BAMBOO FLOORING

Although it's technically a grass, bamboo has much in common with wood. It's the fastest growing plant in the world, and its hardness varies: Strand-woven and end-grain bamboos have superior density and durability, but flat-grain and vertical-grain bamboos are less expensive. Like wood flooring, bamboo can be floating, nailed, or glued, and it can be prefinished or finished in place. It's becoming more sustainable too. Although bamboo was once exclusively imported, some is now being grown in the United States.

Newer on the kitchen front is palm flooring, the product of old palm trees past their coconut-producing years. Lumber from the felled trees is laminated like plywood and is similar to other wood species in both finish and maintenance requirements.

The brick flooring found in this kitchen is in keeping with the rustic beams throughout. Teamed with crisp white cabinetry, it creates a sophisticated country feeling.

more about...
LAMINATE FLOORING

laminate flooring has a clear wear-layer protecting a photo layer that may feature a pattern or color or even have the look of wood, tile, or stone. These two layers are laminated to a high-density fiberboard and a moisture-resistant melamine bottom layer. Today's laminate flooring floats on a smooth underlayment, and the planks or tiles usually fit together tightly with no glue required. Plus it's relatively economical, easy to install, comfortable to stand on, and easy to clean, although the joints are vulnerable to puddled water. You may be surprised at how some laminates look—and feel—like the real thing. For the most realistic woodlike flooring, look for surface embossing that matches the texture you see in the photo layer.

ABOVE Cork flooring is comfortable to stand on for long periods of time and warm to bare feet too. Here, it blends quietly with pale wood cabinets, allowing the rich red walls to take center stage.

Ceramic and stone tiles are classics in the kitchen; they're at once elegant and durable. That said, the downside is that they're hard on your feet and back—and dropped dishes too. Ceramic tile features a glazed layer over a white body, while porcelain, quarry, brick, and stone have color throughout the body, so chips won't be as apparent. Any stone can be cut into tiles; marble, limestone, granite, and slate are the most popular.

All stone tiles (except soapstone) and unglazed tiles require regular sealing to resist staining. An alternative to stone tile, which can be expensive, is glazed ceramic tile that has the look of stone; plus it has the advantage of being waterproof and stain proof.

RIGHT Porcelain tile in this kitchen lends the look of subtle texture to the floor. The large tiles mean there are fewer grout lines too, resulting in less that need to be sealed.

ABOVE Beyond its visual beauty, slate has another appealing attribute—especially in the kitchen. Its uneven surface results in more of a nonslip surface.

walls and ceilings

●●● THE POINT AT WHICH YOU DECIDE ON wall and ceiling materials and finishes will depend on how complex they are. Those that require structural attention must, of course, be designed at the beginning of a kitchen project—a coffered or barrel ceiling, for instance. On the other hand, if it's paint or wallpaper you're considering, selections can wait until a bit further in the process. Still, your overall design scheme will benefit from making all decisions as soon as possible.

Tile, stone, and brick are particularly well suited to walls prone to splashes and splatters, as are washable wallpaper, and glossy or semigloss paints. Patterns and textures can hide scuffs and scrapes. If you find an exquisite tile or stone, but wrapping all the walls is beyond your budget, apply it to one accent wall and treat the rest with a complementary paint color.

While many kitchen ceilings are white, flat, and dotted with recessed can lighting, think of this "fifth wall" as a canvas for creativity. Rustic beams can be added for a country touch, while beadboard paneling can lend a cottage feeling. And color can do wonders for any room. A dark ceiling will feel lower and make the room seem cozier; conversely, a light ceiling will seemingly add height to a space. The bottom line is this: Take the design of your ceiling to new heights.

ABOVE Blue-and-white ceramic tiles add color and pattern to this otherwise all-white kitchen. The pattern is more than just aesthetically pleasing; it hides scratches and scrapes better than solid colors.

LEFT Amid a room full of solid-color elements, from the cabinetry to the stainless-steel countertops and shelves, marble tiles and a marble-topped island lend a touch of much-welcomed pattern, not to mention an air of elegance.

Reclaimed brick, by nature, has variegated colors, and those neutral hues are incorporated throughout this kitchen. The vintage appeal is balanced by more contemporary elements—like the light fixture—creating a comfortable, transitional look.

FACING PAGE Covered in dark wood strips, the vaulted ceiling in this kitchen is a direct reflection of the floor below. Between the two, vertical white-painted planks draw the eye from floor to ceiling.

ABOVE What could have been an ordinary flat white ceiling is anything but. This coffered ceiling is created with dropped beams, establishing an architecturally pleasing grid pattern.

LEFT It's hard to say in this kitchen if the colors started at the floor and worked their way up to the ceiling or if the opposite is true. Either way, both surfaces feature sprightly painted schemes based on the blue of the island.

Instead of being stretched across the entire ceiling, these ceiling beams define the room's core.
The design is strategic, as it still allows space for recessed can lights around the room's perimeter.

LEFT This kitchen is drenched in daylight, which is reflected by the walls and ceiling made of carefully restored planking painted a warm white.

BELOW Subtly patterned red wallpaper adds an element of warmth to this kitchen, but it seemingly changes the dimensions too. A dark color like this makes a ceiling seem lower than it really is, creating a cozier feeling.

windows and lighting

● ● ●

A WELL-LIT KITCHEN CAN DO MORE THAN ILLUMINATE YOUR DAILY tasks; it can brighten your mood as well. The key is to find the right mix of lighting types—whether it's day or night—using a variety of sources. Even if the windows in your kitchen flood the room with natural light, you'll need to supplement it in various ways. If you're chopping vegetables at a prep area, for instance, you'll need task lighting directly above to lessen the chance that you'll cut your finger. And when the family sits down for a meal, some kind of ambient light will let you see what you are eating. Accent lighting most often focuses on specific items, such as a work of art; with more and more of today's kitchens blending into adjacent living areas, accent lighting has become as invaluable in the kitchen as anywhere else in the house. But the bottom line is this: A well-lit kitchen will have a combination of ambient, task, and accent lighting. Finally, to give your lighting plan more flexibility, provide dimmable lighting, switching the various sources of light separately to suit a variety of moods— and to save energy too.

An expansive window teams with skylights to flood this country cottage kitchen with natural light. Ambient light is added at the ceiling level with two rows of decorative bronze downlights.

windows

● ● ● THERE'S SOMETHING WARM AND wonderful about sunshine streaming into a kitchen—literally, to a degree. An abundance of natural light can lessen the need for artificial light sources and also add a heat source; be sure to install shades or curtains, however, to control the amount that you want or need. In temperate weather, open windows can go to work too, providing makeup air to balance the exhaust from a powerful range hood.

Locate windows high enough to bounce the sun's rays off the ceiling for ambient light or position them at countertop level for task lighting. Or you might choose to make them tall enough for both tasks. Another option is to forego wall cabinets on exterior walls in favor of adding more windows. If storage space is an issue, though—and you need the cabinets—consider adding skylights.

RIGHT The windows in this dining area reflect the home's architecture with the transom following the angle of the roofline. The expansive windows provide a beautiful view and make the eating area feel larger in the process.

LEFT Many kitchens have a single window over the sink that provides light and a view beyond. But this kitchen ups the ante with triple windows, multiplying the ambient and task lighting.

A pair of double-hung windows is topped with transoms, creating an extra measure of height. Painting the ceiling white was a strategic decision; sunshine bounces off light colors while it is absorbed by dark hues.

RIGHT An entire window wall at the far end of this kitchen allows an abundance of natural light as well as access to the patio beyond. But a pair of double-hung windows on an adjacent wall does its part too, as do skylights above.

LEFT A window with no mullions is more contemporary in style, but it goes beyond design. The uninterrupted pane of glass also provides a clearer view.

LEFT The vaulted ceiling of this kitchen incorporates ambient lighting in the form of high windows, skylights, and well-placed downlights. A trio of pendant lights hang down over the island, providing ample task lighting too.

lighting

●●● THE THREE TYPES OF LIGHTING THAT make up a beautifully lit room are ambient, task, and accent. **Ambient** lighting provides overall illumination, making it easy to move throughout the room and preventing harsh shadows. In the daytime, natural light can provide much of the ambient light a kitchen needs; at night, ambient light is provided by pendants or chandeliers, recessed lights, track lights, and/or concealed above-cabinet fixtures.

Task lighting illuminates a work area, whether it's a countertop, cooktop, or sink. Undercabinet fixtures of all shapes and sizes provide task lighting, as do pendants, track lights, and recessed can lights. Keep in mind, however, that task lights positioned close to the workspace are more efficient than lights positioned on the ceiling.

Accent lighting illuminates specific objects or it can wash a wall. Track lighting, in-cabinet fixtures, sconces, and recessed fixtures that can be focused can all act as accent lights. Some fixtures fall into the category of decorative lighting too, but they invariably serve a second purpose, whether it is task, ambient, or accent lighting.

A well-thought-out lighting plan illuminates this kitchen, a necessity in the rainy Pacific Northwest. It starts with a skylight running down the middle of the house, and is supplemented in the kitchen with recessed downlights over the work areas and decorative pendants over the eating bar.

gallery

pendants and chandeliers

Pendants and chandeliers can provide ambient or task lighting in a kitchen and an element of style at the same time. Specifically, both are good choices to illuminate a dining table and—if using two or more—an island surface. Choose fixtures that are easy to clean, especially if they're located in the kitchen's work zone. Height is an important consideration too.

As a rule, hang a pendant or chandelier 30 in. above a dining table and 36 in. above a countertop. To allow more ambient light to reach the ceiling, choose a semi-opaque, translucent, or transparent shade. On the other hand, if it's task lighting you're looking for, select an opaque shade that will direct the light downward.

A pair of pendants light up this island, supplementing the room's recessed lighting. Their yellow hue adds an element of sunshine with frosted globes preventing unwelcome glare.

Lantern chandeliers suspended over this island have a lattice design that allows them to emit ambient light from all angles. Their geometric styling is a direct reflection of the pattern found in the coffered ceiling.

A matching chandelier and pendants create a sense of continuity in this kitchen. Still, they have different purposes; the chandelier provides ambient lighting over the dining table while the pendants over the island sink deliver task lighting.

What could be more appropriate for a kitchen than a chandelier with a shade made of flatware? Plenty of ambient light peeks through the spoons and forks, making it just as hardworking as it is decorative.

g a l l e r y

recessed, surface-mounted, and track lighting

Recessed downlights have been a fixture in the kitchen for decades, and for good reason. They come in a wide variety of shapes and sizes, with just as many bulb, baffle, and color options. By spacing downlights close enough together, light pools will overlap on the countertop or floor. (Avoid downlights that allow air and moisture to leak into the ceiling cavity or an attic space; those with IC ratings can be directly covered with insulation.) Adjustable recessed downlights provide drama and make ideal accent lights for art and decorative dishware, but drama may not be a high priority for lighting kitchen workspaces. A ceiling downlight is relatively far from a workspace too, so its bulb must be considerably brighter

to produce the light required for safe and comfortable work, which in turn reduces the overall energy efficiency.

Flush-mounted fixtures, as well as semiflush styles, can provide ambient, task, and accent lighting and can be decorative at the same time. Those with translucent or transparent shades allow light to shine upward to the ceiling and bounce back into the kitchen. Track lighting comes in all shapes and sizes, including high- and low-voltage systems with pendants and adjustable spots. Track lights are not only individually adjustable but can also offer the full range of lighting functions, from ambient to decorative.

LEFT Downlights are strategically placed around this kitchen's perimeter, shining on—and showing off—the marble countertops. Supplementing the lighting scheme are silver globe-shaped pendants, providing task lighting for the island below.

BELOW Downlights are often positioned around a kitchen's perimeter, or situated evenly throughout the space. The downlights in this kitchen, however, are subtly tucked into the room's rustic beams.

FACING PAGE Downlights around the room create ambient light in this kitchen while semiflush-mounted fixtures add an element of task lighting that's decorative at the same time.

LEFT Sconces at this kitchen's ceiling level keep with the room's contemporary scheme, casting light downward onto the honed slate countertops. Meanwhile, an infinitely adjustable cable-rail system adds another light source to the space.

This kitchen's soaring ceiling is punctuated by clerestory windows, bouncing light off the white walls as well as the pale wood cabinetry below. Recessed downlights and decorative pendants do their part to illuminate the space once night falls.

more about...
LIGHTING CONTROLS AND RECEPTACLES

automated control systems allow you to program in many lighting scenarios, any of which you can call up by touching a pad. While these systems are convenient, they can also be expensive, depending on how complex they are. The alternatives include everything from rotary, slide, or touch dimmer controls to wireless systems.

Receptacles need not be white boxes that seem randomly strewn throughout your kitchen. You might, for instance, tuck plug molding—a continuous strip of outlets—under a wall cabinet or along the backsplash, or simply stack multiple receptacles in one convenient (but not glaringly obvious) place. Islands require receptacles too, but these are more of a challenge to play down. A two-height island offers a perfect backsplash location for island receptacles; a hollowed-out island leg can also make a good home for them.

ABOVE A trio of stainless-steel-shrouded pendants are suspended over this island, creating overlapping pools of light perfectly suited to the tasks performed here. A matching fixture is positioned over the sink, creating a sense of design continuity.

ABOVE To create a stream-lined look in this kitchen, one uninterrupted by receptacles, these homeowners found a way to be creative with their placement—tucked behind a drawer front.

LEFT A row of these bronze fixtures, which provide ambient lighting, marches down each side of this kitchen. Their decorative appeal draws the eye upward, making the room seem taller.

m o r e   a b o u t . . .

LIGHTBULBS

ightbulbs have come, well, light-years in terms of their efficiency and longevity. Incandescent bulbs—the one Thomas Edison perfected—have long been the bulb of choice. They've been appreciated for the warm light they cast, but they are low efficiency and generate high heat. (Only 10% of the energy used by these bulbs produces light while the excess escapes as heat; thus they are slowly being phased out of production.) Halogen, also known as tungsten-halogen, is more energy efficient and long-lived than standard incandescents.

Compact florescent lamps (CFLs) can fit into standard lamp bases, using about 70% less energy than incandescents and lasting years longer. Plus the cost difference is minimal; CFLs,

on the average, cost only a dollar more per bulb than their incandescent counterparts. CFLs do contain a small amount of mercury, however, meaning it's important to clean up a broken bulb quickly and safely. In addition, they need to be recycled and not tossed with the rest of your kitchen trash.

What sets LEDs (light-emitting diodes) apart from incandescents and CFLs is that they last up to five times longer than any comparable bulb. Until recently, that efficiency has come at a high price; a single LED bulb once cost $50 or more. Today, however, the average price of an LED bulb runs between $5 and $8.

•lighting wall cabinets

Because they bring the light source so close to the surface, undercabinet fixtures can provide ideal task lighting for working countertops. They're also easy to conceal behind the cabinet case or door. But undercabinet lights can provide ambient light too, especially if the backsplash and countertop are light in tone and softly reflective. Keep in mind that undercabinet lights will be reflected more on a polished countertop; select a honed or brushed material for a softer reflected light. To avoid a harsh glare, install undercabinet fixtures along the bottom front inside edge of wall cabinets.

You'll find several types of undercabinet fixtures on the market. Halogen puck lights are bright white and easy to install, but they generate a lot of heat. Shallow fluorescent tubes are long-lasting, energy-efficient, and inexpensive. Xenon tubes are cooler running and longer-lived than halogen and have a warmer tint than some fluorescent tubes. And small light-emitting diode (LED) undercabinet fixtures are long-lasting and energy-efficient; though relatively expensive in the past, they're becoming less so.

By adding accent lighting to the interiors of glass-door wall cabinets, you can create a dramatic ambience. In addition, if there are glass shelves inside, the drama is elevated because the light inside is reflected from more angles.

ABOVE To showcase art glass and special serving pieces in this kitchen, downlights set into a soffit shine on their respective shelves. The subtlety of the frosted-glass doors between them provides contrast, making the objects seem to shine brighter.

FACING PAGE TOP Downlights are set into this kitchen's shelves as well as the hood of the nearby range. The pools of light add interest, appearing to reflect the wall's chevronlike pattern.

FACING PAGE BOTTOM Undercabinet lighting in this kitchen highlights the asymmetrical wood shelves while illuminating the countertop below. The result is task lighting on both sides of the range that also creates ambient lighting.

photo credits

pp. ii-iii: Eric Roth, design: Hutker Architects

p. vi: trentbellphotography, design: Maine Home & Design (top left); Mark Lohman, design: Alison Kandler Interior Design (top right); Tria Giovan (bottom left); Ryann Ford (bottom right)

p. 1: Tria Giovan, design: Chandos Interiors (top left); Tria Giovan, design: Courtney Hill Interiors (top center); Ken Gutmaker, design: kda-berkeley.com (top right); Susan Teare, design: wanta-architect pllc (bottom left); Mark Lohman, design: Alison Kandler Interior Design (bottom right)

pp. 2-3: Olson Photographic, design: Joe Currie (left); Tria Giovan, design: Marshall Watson (center); Tria Giovan, design: Brady Design (right)

CHAPTER 1

p. 4: trentbellphotography, design: Maine Home & Design

p. 6: Mark Lohman, design: Brown Design & Development and Dugally Oberfeld

p. 7: Mark Lohman, design: Audrey Graham Kennedy (top); Tria Giovan, architect: Louise Brooks (bottom left); Hulya Kolabas, design: Mar Silver Design (bottom right)

p. 8: trentbellphotography, design: Bowley Builders

p. 9: Ryann Ford, design: Amity Worrel, builder: Don Tenney, architect: Sherri Ancipink (top); David Duncan Livingston (bottom)

p. 10: David Duncan Livingston (top); Tria Giovan, design: Brady Design (bottom)

p. 11: Mark Lohman, design: Laurie Haefele Design (top); Eric Roth, design: Heartwood Kitchens (bottom)

p. 12: Eric Roth, design: Adams and Beasley Design

p. 13: Eric Roth, design: Mathew Cecil Design (top); David Duncan Livingston (bottom)

p. 14: Ryann Ford, design: Tim Cuppett Architects (left); Mark Lohman, design: Caroline Burke Designs & Associates (right)

p. 15: Ryann Ford, design: Michael Deane Homes (mdh.com), Elizabeth Stanley Design (www.elizabethstanleydesign.com) (top)

p. 16: Hulya Kolabas (top); Rachel Martin, design: Design Galleria Kitchen and Bath Studio (bottom)

p. 17: Ryann Ford, design: Heather Scott Home & Design (www.heatherscotthome. com), Silverton Custom Homes (www. silvertoncustomhomes.com) (top); Eric Roth, design: Martha's Vineyard Interior Design (bottom)

p. 18: Tria Giovan, design: Bobby McAlpine (top); Mark Lohman (bottom)

p. 19: Mark Lohman, design: Alison Kandler Interior Design

p. 20: Ken Gutmaker, design: eggfarkarch. com (top); Ryann Ford, design: Stuart Sampley Architect (stuartsampleyarchitect. com) (bottom)

p. 21: Hulya Kolabas, design: Guillaume Gentet Design (top); Laurie Black, design: Pacific Design (bottom)

p. 22: Andrea Rugg Photography/Collinstock, design: Otogawa-Anschel Design + Build (top); Olson Photographic, design: Hemmingway Construction (bottom)

p. 23: Andrea Rugg Photography/Collinstock, design: Peterssen/Keller Architecture (top right); Chipper Hatter, design: Nicely Done Kitchens/Evelyn Nicely (bottom)

p. 24: Chipper Hatter, design: Cabinet Factory Outlet Plus/Howland Boyer

p. 25: Ken Gutmaker, design: www. andrerothblattarchitecture.com (top); Eric Roth, design: Jamie Florence Designs (bottom)

p. 26: Andrea Rugg Photography, design: Rolf Lokensgard Architecture

p. 27: Tria Giovan, design: Courtney Hill Interiors

p. 28: Eric Roth, design: Amy McFaddin Design (top); David Duncan Livingston (bottom)

p. 29: Randy O'Rourke, design: Knight Associates

p. 30: Eric Roth, design: Hutker Architects

p. 31: Hulya Kolabas (top); Susan Teare © The Taunton Press (bottom)

p. 32: Ryann Ford, design: Fern Santini (www.fernsantini.com), Architect: Gary Furman (www.fkarchitects.net)

p. 33: Laurie Black, design: Reveal Architecture + Interiors (top); Eric Roth, design: Martha's Vineyard Interior Design (bottom)

CHAPTER 2

p. 34: Mark Lohman, design: Alison Kandler Interior Design

p. 36: Eric Roth, design: Heartwood Kitchens

p. 37: David Duncan Livingston (top); Randy O'Rourke, design: Knight Associates (bottom left & right)

p. 38: Mark Lohman (left); Mark Lohman, design: Audrey Graham Kennedy (right)

p. 39: Laurie Black, design: Gaspars Construction (top); Andrea Rugg Photography/Collinstock, design: Casa Verde Design (bottom)

p. 40: Eric Roth, design: Jewett Farms Kitchen Design

p. 41: David Duncan Livingston (top left); Mark Lohman (top right); Andrea Rugg Photography/Collinstock (bottom)

p. 42: Olson Photographic, design: Joe Currie (top); Mark Lohman, design: Alison Kandler Interior Design (bottom)

p. 43: Chipper Hatter, design: Home Improvements Group/Chris Dreith

p. 44: Eric Roth, design: Mathew Cecil Design (top); Mark Lohman, design: Alison Kandler Interior Design (bottom)

p. 45: Mark Lohman, design: Laurie Haefele Design

p. 46: Eric Roth, design: Catherine and McClure Interiors (left); David Duncan Livingston (right)

p. 47: Tria Giovan, design: Marshall Watson

p. 48: Tria Giovan, design: Heather Chadduck

p. 49: Stacy Bass, design: Yvonne Claveloux (top); Undine Prohl, design: RCH Studio (bottom left & right)

CHAPTER 3

p. 50: Tria Giovan

p. 52: Mark Lohman, design: Audrey Graham Kennedy

p. 53: Mark Lohman, design: Alison Kandler Interior Design (all)

p. 108: Chipper Hatter, design: Home Improvements Group/Chris Dreith (left); Eric Roth, design: Cummings Architects (right)

CHAPTER 5

p. 110: Tria Giovan, design: Chandos Interiors

p. 112: Rachel Martin, design: Design Galleria Kitchen and Bath Studio (left); Ryann Ford, design: Fern Santini (www.fernsantini.com), architect: Gary Furman (www.fkarchitects.net) (right)

p. 113: Ryann Ford, design: Poteet Architects (www.poteetarchitects.com)

p. 114: Eric Roth, design: Jamie Florence Designs (top left); Mark Lohman (top right); Undine Prohl, design: Quincy Jones (bottom left); Mark Lohman (bottom right)

p. 115: Mark Lohman, design: Alison Kandler Interior Design

p. 116: Ryann Ford, design: Sally Wheat Interiors (www.sallywheatinteriors.com)

p. 117: Undine Prohl, design: Taalman Koch Architecture (top); Eric Roth, design: Martha's Vineyard Interior Design (bottom left); Ryann Ford, design: Lucas Eilers Design Associates (www.lucaseilers.com) (bottom right)

p. 118: Ryann Ford, design: Tim Cuppett Architects

p. 119: Hulya Kolabas, design: Mar Silver Design (top left); Tria Giovan, design: Heather Chadduck (bottom left & right)

p. 120: Andrea Rugg Photography

p. 121: David Duncan Livingston (left & right)

p. 122: Olson Photographic, design: Laura Cochran (top); Mark Lohman, design: Alison Kandler Interior Design (bottom)

p. 123: Susan Teare, design: Studio III Architecture (top); Randy O'Rourke, design: Knight Associates (bottom)

p. 124: Andrea Rugg Photography/Collinstock, design: (left); Mark Lohman, design: Alison Kandler Interior Design (top right); Mark Lohman, design: Caroline Burke Designs & Associates (bottom right)

p. 125: Laurie Black, design: Pacific Design

p. 126: Tria Giovan (left); Chipper Hatter, design: Home Improvements Group/Chris Dreith (right)

p. 127: Mark Lohman, design: Alison Kandler Interior Design (left & right)

CHAPTER 6

p. 128: Tria Giovan, design: Courtney Hill Interiors

p. 130: Ryann Ford, design: Lucas Eilers Design Associates (www.lucaseilers.com)

p. 131: Tria Giovan, design: Brady Design (top); Jo-Ann Richards, design: The Sky Is the Limit Design (bottom)

p. 132: Laurie Black, design: Amy Baker Interior Design

p. 133: Andrea Rugg Photography/Collinstock, design: Otogawa-Anschel Design + Build (top left); Susan Teare © The Taunton Press (bottom left); Mark Lohman, design: Caroline Burke Designs & Associates (right)

p. 134: John Gruen © The Taunton Press

p. 135: trentbellphotography, design: Priestly + Associates Architecture (top); Eric Roth, design: Feinmann Build and Design (bottom)

p. 136: David Duncan Livingston

p. 137: Ryann Ford, design: Anabel Interiors (www.anabelinteriors.com) (top left); Mark Lohman, design: Laurie Haefele Design (top right); Ken Gutmaker, design: www.andrerothblattarchitecture.com (bottom)

p. 138: Eric Roth, design: Amy McFaddin Design (top left); Undine Prohl, design: Quincy Jones (bottom left); Stacy Bass, design: Carl Thompson and Jessica Waldman (right)

p. 140: Tria Giovan

p. 141: Mark Lohman (top left & bottom left); Eric Roth, design: Jeanne Upton Interiors (right)

p. 142: Olson Photographic, design: A Matter of Style (top left); Mark Lohman (top right); David Duncan Livingston, design: Justine Macfee (jmacfee@macfeedesign.com) (bottom)

p. 143: Mark Lohman, design: Audrey Graham Kennedy

p. 144: Susan Teare, design: Cushman Design Group (left); Tria Giovan, design: Ray Booth (right)

p. 146: Eric Roth, design: Feinmann Build and Design (top left); Eric Roth, design: Jewett Farms Kitchen Design (top right); Brian Vanden Brink © The Taunton Press (bottom)

p. 147: Mark Lohman

p. 148: Mark Lohman, design: Audrey Graham Kennedy

p. 149: Ryann Ford, design: Amity Worrel, builder: Don Tenney, architect: Sherri Ancipink (top); Eric Roth, design: Metropolitan Kitchens (bottom)

p. 150: Stacy Bass, design: Jennifer Downing (top); Susan Teare, design: Burlington Marble & Granite, Inc. (bottom)

p. 152: Mark Lohman, design: Alison Kandler Interior Design

p. 153: Randy O'Rourke, design: Frank Shirley Architects (top); Mark Lohman, design: Alison Kandler Interior Design (bottom)

p. 154: Randy O'Rourke, design: Knight Associates

p. 155: Ken Gutmaker, design: kda-berkeley.com

p. 156: Jo-Ann Richards, design: Smith Designs

p. 158: David Duncan Livingston (left); Tria Giovan (right)

p. 159: Mark Lohman, design: Audrey Graham Kennedy

p. 160: Mark Lohman, design: Caroline Burke Designs & Associates (top); Eric Roth, design: Meyer and Meyer Architects (bottom)

p. 161: Olson Photographic, design: Joe Currie

CHAPTER 7

p. 162: Ken Gutmaker, design: kda-berkeley.com

p. 164: Eric Roth, design: Keith Lichtman Design (left); Mark Lohman (right)

p. 165: Eric Roth, design: Deborah Ferrand/Dressing Rooms Interiors

p. 166: Chipper Hatter, design: Nicely Done Kitchens/Evelyn Nicely

p. 167: Eric Roth, design: Dalusso Design (left); Mark Lohman, design: Caroline Burke Designs & Associates (right)

p. 168: Mark Lohman, design: Alison Kandler Interior Design

p. 169: Mark Lohman, design: Alison Kandler Interior Design (top left & top right); Mark Lohman (bottom left); Ryann Ford, design: Heather Scott Home & Design (www.heatherscotthome.com), Silverton Custom Homes (www.silvertoncustomhomes.com) (bottom right)

p. 170: Randy O'Rourke, design: Knight Associates

p. 171: Jo-Ann Richards, design: The Sky Is the Limit Design (top); Mark Lohman, design: Caroline Burke Designs & Associates (bottom)

p. 172: Mark Lohman, design: Janet Lohman Interior Design (left); Eric Roth, design: Feinmann Build and Design (right)

p. 173: Olson Photographic, design: Dan Vanente, Complete Construction

p. 174: Olson Photographic, design: Putnam Kitchens (left); Chipper Hatter, design: Solomon Interiors/Jan Solomon (right)

p. 176: Mark Lohman

p. 177: Chipper Hatter, design: Nicely Done Kitchens/Evelyn Nicely (top); Mark Lohman (bottom)

p. 178: Ryann Ford (top left); Andrea Rugg Photography/Collinstock (top right); Rachel Martin, design: Design Galleria Kitchen and Bath Studio (bottom left); Olson Photographic, design: Robik Glantz Builders (bottom right)

p. 179: Tria Giovan, design: Phillip Sides

p. 180: Mark Lohman (left); Mark Lohman, design: Caroline Burke Designs & Associates (right)

p. 181: Chipper Hatter, design: Roomscapes/ Debbie Nassetta

p. 182: Undine Prohl, design: Quincy Jones (left); trentbellphotography, design: Blue Heron (right)

p. 183: Mark Lohman, design: Alison Kandler Interior Design (left); Mark Lohman, design: Audrey Graham Kennedy (right)

p. 184: Randy O'Rourke, design: Knight Associates (left); Olson Photographic, design: Village Square Properties (right)

p. 185: Mark Lohman, design: Audrey Graham Kennedy

CHAPTER 8

p. 186: Susan Teare, design: wanta-architect pllc

p. 188: Mark Lohman, design: Alison Kandler Interior Design

p. 189: Mark Lohman, design: Audrey Graham Kennedy (top left); Randy O'Rourke, design: Knight Associates (top right); Ryann Ford, design: Tim Cuppett Architects (bottom)

p. 190: Jo-Ann Richards, design: The House Dressing Company (left); Mark Lohman, design: Alison Kandler Interior Design (right)

p. 191: Brian Vanden Brink © The Taunton Press

p. 192: Chipper Hatter, design: Ourso Design/Richard Ourso

p. 193: Eric Roth, design: Britta Design (top left); Mark Lohman, design: Caroline Burke Designs & Associates (bottom left); Mark Lohman (right)

p. 194: Hulya Kolabas, design: Mar Silver Design (left); Ryann Ford, design: Amity Worrel, builder: Don Tenney, architect: Sherri Ancipink (right)

p. 195: Tria Giovan, design: Kevin Spearman

p. 196: Hulya Kolabas, design: Mar Silver Design

p. 197: Mark Lohman, design: Audrey Graham Kennedy (top); Tria Giovan (bottom)

p. 198: Eric Roth, design: Hutker Architects

p. 199: John Gruen © The Taunton Press (top); Olson Photographic, design: VAS Construction (bottom)

CHAPTER 9

p. 200: Mark Lohman, design: Alison Kandler Interior Design

p. 202: Ryann Ford, design: Amity Worrel, builder: Don Tenney, architect: Sherri Ancipink (left); Randy O'Rourke, design: Knight Associates (right)

p. 203: Tria Giovan, architect: Austin Patterson Disston

p. 204: Laurie Black, design: Gaspars Construction (left); Tria Giovan, design: Martha McCully (right)

p. 205: Mark Lohman, design: Caroline Burke Designs & Associates (bottom)

p. 206: Denis Hill © The Taunton Press

p. 207: Mark Lohman, design: Alison Kandler Interior Design (top left); Mark Lohman, design: Audrey Graham Kennedy (top right); Randy O'Rourke, design: Knight Associates (bottom left); Eric Roth © The Taunton Press (bottom right)

p. 208: Eric Roth, design: Heartwood Kitchens

p. 209: Hulya Kolabas (top); Randy O'Rourke, design: Knight Associates (bottom left); Eric Roth, design: Jewett Farms Kitchen Design (bottom right)

p. 210: Eric Roth, design: Britta Design

p. 211: Mark Lohman (top left); Jo-Ann Richards, design: The Sky Is the Limit Design (top right); Mark Lohman (bottom)

p. 212: Eric Roth, design: Leslie Fine Interiors

p. 213: Eric Roth, design: Jeff Swanson, Renovation Planning, LLC (top); Ken Gutmaker, design: www.at-six.com (bottom)

If you like this book, you'll love *Fine Homebuilding.*

Read *Fine Homebuilding* Magazine:

Get eight issues, including our two annual design issues, *Houses* and *Kitchens & Baths*, plus FREE tablet editions. Packed with expert advice and skill-building techniques, every issue provides the latest information on quality building and remodeling.

Subscribe today at:
FineHomebuilding.com/4Sub

Discover our *Fine Homebuilding* Online Store:

It's your destination for premium resources from America's best builders: how-to and design books, DVDs, videos, special interest publications, and more.

Visit today at:
FineHomebuilding.com/4More

Get our FREE *Fine Homebuilding* eNewsletter:

Keep up with the current best practices, the newest tools, and the latest materials, plus free tips and advice from *Fine Homebuilding* editors.

Sign up, it's free:
FineHomebuilding.com/4Newsletter

Become a FineHomebuilding.com member:

Join to enjoy unlimited access to premium content and exclusive benefits, including: 1,400+ articles; 350 tip, tool, and technique videos; our how-to video project series; over 1,600 field-tested tips; monthly giveaways; tablet editions; contests; special offers; and more.

Discover more information online:
FineHomebuilding.com/4Join

Taunton